Budgeting for Impulse Spending

Stop Overspending With One Habit That Actually Works

Odette Amaral

First edition, 2026

Published by Odette Amaral

Contents

Chapter 1: The Leak in the Bucket

In January 2019, Marie Kondo appeared on millions of American television screens holding a folded t-shirt like a baby bird. Her Netflix show promised transformation through gratitude: thank your possessions, discard the rest, change your life. Within weeks, Goodwill donation centers were overwhelmed. Six months later, most of those same people were buying it all back.

Six months later, most of those same people were buying it all back.

Not the exact same items, obviously. But the pattern held. New throw pillows. Different organizational bins. Another set of kitchen gadgets that would solve everything *this* time. The purge-and-purchase cycle that defines modern consumer life, playing out in living rooms across America like a sitcom nobody finds funny anymore.

I know this because I watched it happen to my sister. And because I did it myself.

The worst part wasn't the money, though that stung. It was the creeping realization that I had no idea where my paycheck actually went. I earned a decent living as a consultant. I wasn't buying yachts or designer handbags. I just... ran out of money. Every month. Like clockwork.

You know the feeling. That moment at the end of the month when you check your account balance and think, "Wait, where did it all go?" You scan back through transactions looking for the culprit—some big, obvious expense you can blame. But there isn't one. Just a long scroll of small charges, each one individually defensible, collectively devastating.

A coffee here. Lunch there. That thing Amazon suggested. The subscription you forgot to cancel. Another subscription you definitely meant to use more. Parking. A book you haven't read. Socks, because the dryer apparently eats them. A phone case. A better phone case. Something for the kitchen that seemed essential at 11 PM on a Tuesday.

Death by a thousand purchases.

Sarah Blakely, the founder of Spanx, tells a story about selling fax machines door-to-door in her twenties. She was terrible at it. Made almost no money. But she learned something that would later make her a billionaire: people don't buy products. They buy the feeling they think the product will give them.

That's the trap. We're not actually shopping for things. We're shopping for emotions. Relief from boredom. A buffer against stress. The brief dopamine hit that comes from clicking "buy now" when everything else feels out of control.

I figured this out the hard way.

It was a Tuesday morning. I'd been up late working on a client presentation that had gone sideways—one of those projects where every stakeholder wants something different and you're trying to thread a needle while blindfolded. Around midnight, exhausted and wired on coffee, I started browsing Amazon. Just to decompress, I told myself. Just to look.

By Thursday morning, six boxes were stacked by my front door.

Noise-canceling headphones. I already owned two pairs. A Japanese woodblock print I'd seen for maybe thirty seconds before buying. A portable espresso maker, despite having a perfectly good one upstairs. Calligraphy pens. Organic matcha powder. And—I am not making this up—a miniature Zen garden.

Total damage: $387.

I stood there in my kitchen, staring at this cardboard monument to poor impulse control, and something clicked. This wasn't about treating myself. I wasn't rewarding hard work or practicing self-care or any of the other stories I'd been telling myself. This was avoidance. Pure and simple. I was upset about the client situation, anxious about whether I'd nailed the presentation, worried about my professional reputation. And instead of sitting with those uncomfortable feelings, I'd medicated them with one-click purchasing.

Emotional avoidance with a credit card.

Here's what I wish someone had told me years earlier: willpower is not the solution. Willpower is what you try when you don't understand the problem.

Let me explain.

For most of human history, acquiring anything required real effort. You wanted meat? Go kill something. You wanted shelter? Build it yourself or trade something valuable for it. You wanted pretty much anything? Get ready to work, negotiate, or wait.

That friction was built into the system. It created natural pause points. Time to reconsider whether you really needed something. Whether it was worth the effort.

Now? Anything you can imagine is available instantly, delivered to your door within hours. Sometimes within minutes. This is not a small change. This is a fundamental restructuring of how humans interact with resources, and our brains have not caught up.

We're running Stone Age software on a smartphone. And it shows.

The Harvard psychologist Daniel Gilbert studies how humans predict what will make them happy. His research shows we're remarkably bad at it. We consistently overestimate how much pleasure we'll get from acquiring things and underestimate how quickly that pleasure fades. But knowing this doesn't help. We make the same mistakes over and over, trapped in what Gilbert calls the "impact bias."

You see the new gadget. Your brain floods with anticipation—imagining how much better your life will be once you own it. You buy it. You feel great for maybe an hour, maybe a day. Then it becomes part of the background. Just another thing you own. The pleasure evaporates, but the charge on your credit card remains.

This isn't a character flaw. It's neuroscience. Your brain is literally designed to seek novelty and immediate rewards. In the ancestral environment, that made sense. Food was scarce. If you found a berry bush, you ate as many berries as possible because you didn't know when you'd eat again. Delayed gratification could mean starvation.

But we're not foraging for berries anymore. We're scrolling through Instagram at 2 AM, and every ad is engineered by people who understand your brain better than you do.

They've run the A/B tests. They know which colors make you click. Which words trigger urgency. How to create artificial scarcity ("Only 3 left in stock!") and social proof ("12,847 people bought this today"). They've gamified shopping, turned it into a dopamine slot machine where every click might deliver that little hit of pleasure.

And it works.

Not because you're weak. Because you're human.

I worked with a client named Amelia—a marketing manager at a tech company, pulling down six figures. Smart, capable, organized in every area of her life except one. She color-coded her closet. She never missed a workout. She hit every deadline at work.

But her bank account was chaos.

She'd download a budgeting app, track expenses for exactly one week, then abandon it in frustration. The problem wasn't that she couldn't understand the app. The problem was that seeing where her money went made her feel terrible. Ashamed. Out of control.

Better not to look.

When we finally sat down and went through a month of transactions together, she was quiet for a long time. Then she said, "I earn more than my parents ever did. Combined. How is there nothing left?"

The answer was there in the spreadsheet. Hundreds of small charges. Seven-dollar lattes. Candles. Books she hadn't read. Makeup she didn't need. Instagram impulse buys. Subscription services she'd forgotten existed. None of it felt significant in the moment. All of it added up to roughly 20% of her monthly income just... vanishing.

That's the thing about leaks. They're small enough to ignore individually. But water doesn't care about your intentions. It just keeps dripping.

You're probably thinking: "Okay, but I'm not that bad. I don't have a spending problem. I just... sometimes get caught up in the moment."

Let me ask you this: How many subscription services are you paying for right now? Not the ones you actively use. All of them. The streaming service you signed up for to watch one show. The meditation app you used twice. The meal kit delivery that seemed like a great idea in January. The premium version of that thing you could definitely use the free version of.

Go ahead. Check your bank statement. I'll wait.

Found a few you forgot about? Most people do. The subscription economy is brilliant specifically because it bypasses the pain of purchasing. You sign up once, and then the charges just... happen. Automatically. Forever. Or until you notice and take action, which requires more activation energy than most people can muster on a random Tuesday.

This is what I mean by a design problem.

The system is built to extract money from you with minimum friction and maximum psychological manipulation. And then we're shocked when it works.

Marcus Aurelius, the Roman emperor who moonlighted as a Stoic philosopher, wrote in his *Meditations*: "If you are distressed by anything external, the pain is not due to the thing itself, but to your estimate of it; and this you have the power to revoke at any moment."

Beautiful sentiment. Terrible financial advice.

Because the "external thing" in this case is a billion-dollar marketing industry that has spent decades perfecting the art of separating you from your money. You're not fighting your own lack of discipline. You're fighting teams of behavioral psychologists, data scientists, and UX designers whose literal job is to make you click "buy."

That's not a fair fight. And you can't win it with willpower alone.

I learned this watching another client—Ben, a software engineer in Seattle. He was tracking everything in a budgeting app. Following all the conventional advice. And still, every month, he'd overspend on video games and tech gadgets.

When I asked him why, he had to think about it. "I guess... I don't even enjoy them that much? I'll buy a new game, play it for a few hours, then just feel empty. Then I buy another one."

"What are you feeling right before you buy them?" I asked.

Long pause. "Bored. Or stressed about work. Like I need something to look forward to."

There it was. He wasn't buying games. He was buying the promise of excitement. An escape from monotony. The purchases were a symptom, not the disease.

This is where most budgeting advice falls apart. It treats impulse spending as a math problem when it's actually an emotional one. The traditional approach says: "Make a budget. Stick to it. Use willpower." Which is like telling someone with insomnia to "just sleep."

Thanks. Super helpful.

The real question isn't "How do I stop spending money?" The real question is "What need am I trying to meet with this purchase, and is there a better way to meet it?"

Ben wasn't actually interested in video games. He was interested in feeling something other than the low-grade anxiety that came with his job. Once he identified that, we could address it directly. He started rock climbing. Joined a D&D; group. Took up woodworking. None of these were free, but they cost less than his gaming habit and actually delivered the feeling he was chasing.

More importantly, they required showing up. Being present. You can't half-ass rock climbing. You can't scroll through a D&D; session on autopilot. These activities demanded engagement, which is what his brain actually needed.

The impulse buying dropped off on its own. Because the void he'd been trying to fill with purchases was finally getting filled by something real.

Now, I know what you're thinking: "Great, so I just need to solve all my emotional problems and then I'll stop spending money? Fantastic. Let me just clear my schedule for the next five years of therapy."

No. I'm not saying you need to achieve enlightenment before you can fix your budget. I'm saying that pretending impulse spending is purely rational—something you can think your way out of—is doomed to fail.

You need a system. Not more discipline. A system that works *with* your brain instead of against it.

Think about your finances like a bucket. Water (money) flows in from your income. But the bucket has leaks—those impulse purchases, forgotten subscriptions, mindless little expenses. Traditional budgeting tries to plug every leak through sheer force of will. You tell yourself "no" over and over, trying to be strong enough to resist every temptation.

How's that working out?

For most people: not great. Because you can't maintain that level of vigilance indefinitely. Eventually you get tired. Or stressed. Or something goes wrong. And when your willpower is depleted, all those carefully plugged leaks burst open at once. You "fall off the wagon" and binge-spend, then feel so guilty that you just... stop tracking altogether.

The shame spiral begins. And shame is rocket fuel for more impulse spending because now you're not just bored or stressed—you're also disappointed in yourself.

What if instead of trying to eliminate the leaks, we just... made them smaller? More manageable?

What if we acknowledged that you're going to make impulse purchases—because you're human, and humans seek pleasure and avoid pain—and built that into the system from the start?

This is the approach that actually works. Not restriction. Redirection.

You create a designated space for impulse spending. A "fun fund" or micro-budget or whatever you want to call it. A fixed amount each month that you can spend on absolutely anything without guilt. The miniature Zen garden? Fine. The artisanal cheese? Go for it. The concert tickets? Enjoy.

But once that money's gone, it's gone. You don't get to raid other categories. You don't get to tell yourself "I'll pay myself back next month" (you won't). The boundary is firm, but within that boundary, you're free.

This might sound like giving yourself permission to fail. It's not. It's giving yourself permission to be human.

And here's the interesting part: when you remove the guilt and shame from impulse spending, the compulsive quality often fades. It stops being forbidden fruit. It's just... money you've allocated for things that make you happy. Sometimes you'll spend it. Sometimes you won't. Either way, you're making a choice instead of being controlled by the impulse.

Jocko Willink, the former Navy SEAL who wrote *Extreme Ownership*, talks about "discipline equals freedom." It sounds paradoxical, but it's not. Structure creates space. Boundaries create possibility. When you know exactly how much you can spend on impulse purchases without derailing your goals, you're free to enjoy those purchases without the creeping dread that you're sabotaging your future.

The flip side is also true: chaos equals constraint. When everything is permitted, nothing feels safe. You're always one bad day away from blowing up your budget. That low-level financial anxiety follows you everywhere, poisoning even legitimate purchases because you're never sure if you can afford them.

I see this all the time. People who earn plenty of money but feel broke. Because they have no system. No boundaries. Just a vague sense of dread and a credit card balance that keeps climbing.

So where do you start?

Not with cutting. With measuring.

For the next week—seven days—track every single purchase. Every coffee. Every parking fee. Every app, snack, subscription, impulse buy. Don't change your behavior. Don't judge yourself. Just observe.

Write it down. Spreadsheet, notebook, app, whatever works. The medium doesn't matter. The awareness does.

Because you cannot manage what you cannot measure. And most people have no idea where their money actually goes. They have a general sense, maybe. They know the big stuff—rent, car payment, insurance. But the small stuff? The leaks? Those are invisible until you force yourself to look.

When Amelia did this exercise, she was shocked. Not by any single purchase, but by the cumulative weight. The $4 coffee didn't matter. The fifteen $4 coffees mattered. The $12 lunch was fine. The twenty $12 lunches were a problem. Individually rational. Collectively unsustainable.

She'd been here before, of course. She'd tracked expenses in the past. But previously, she'd done it with the goal of shaming herself into better behavior. This time was different. This time, the goal was just to see. To gather data. No judgment.

That shift mattered more than she expected.

Because when you track expenses as a form of self-punishment, you're motivated to stop as soon as possible. The awareness hurts. You don't want to confront your failures every day. So you quit.

But when you track expenses as research—as gathering information about your own patterns and triggers—it becomes interesting instead of painful. You start noticing things. "Huh, I always buy something random on Thursday afternoons. I wonder why?" (Turns out, Thursday was her worst day at work. The impulse purchases were a coping mechanism.)

Once you see the pattern, you can interrupt it. Not through willpower, but through design. Maybe Thursday afternoons you go for a walk instead of scrolling Instagram. Maybe you text a friend. Maybe you just... notice the urge and let it pass without acting on it.

But you can't do any of that if you don't know the pattern exists.

So: track everything for seven days. Then look at what you found. Not with judgment. With curiosity.

Where is the water going? Which leaks are biggest? And more importantly: *Why* are those leaks there?

Are you spending money when you're stressed? Bored? Lonely? Trying to impress someone? Filling time because you don't know what else to do?

The answer will be different for everyone. But the question is the same: What am I actually buying with this money?

Because I promise you, it's not the miniature Zen garden.

Your spending isn't a hole you can patch once and walk away from—it's a bucket with a slow leak, and the leak is the pattern, not the purchase.

Marie Kondo's audience purged their closets and bought it all back. But they didn't wake up one morning and decide to be wasteful. Something was driving the leak.

Chapter 2: Understanding the Impulse Loop

I was standing in front of thirty people teaching a workshop on impulse spending when my phone buzzed. Order confirmation: $4.99 for MealFlow Premium, a meal-planning app I'd just downloaded while waiting for the projector to warm up. Third one that month. I hadn't opened either of the previous two past day two.

I kept talking, kept clicking through my carefully prepared deck about impulse spending, and felt that familiar wash of sheepish recognition. Here I was, literally teaching people how to stop buying things they don't need, while my phone buzzed with proof I was still doing it myself.

That's the thing about impulse spending that nobody wants to admit: it doesn't care how smart you are, how educated, how aware. You can understand the problem intellectually and still find your thumb hovering over "Complete Purchase" at 11 PM on a Tuesday.

Because impulse spending isn't a willpower problem. It's a design problem.

We've built a financial system that assumes we're always making rational choices, then acts surprised when our lizard brain hits "buy now" at 11 PM. We get sold the story that disciplined people simply resist temptation, that the solution is to white-knuckle your way past every ad, every sale email, every targeted Instagram post that somehow knows you've been thinking about new running shoes.

But willpower is a terrible long-term strategy. It's like trying to hold back a flood with a teacup—sure, you might manage for a while, but eventually your arm gets tired and the water wins.

What's actually happening isn't a failure of strength. It's a loop. A predictable, measurable, neurological pattern that your brain gets stuck in. And the first step toward regaining control isn't to try harder. It's to understand how the loop works.

Let me show you what the loop looks like in real life.

Sarah Chen is a graphic designer in Seattle. Thirty-two, freelance, does branding work for tech startups. Good at her job. Makes decent money. And every time she opens her inbox and sees a sale email from Everlane or Reformation, she feels something shift in her chest.

Not excitement, exactly. More like... possibility. Like maybe this time, this dress, this particular arrangement of fabric and thread will be the thing that makes her feel put-together when she's on a client video call. The thing that makes her look like the kind of designer who has her life figured out.

She's sitting at her desk when the email comes in. It's 2 PM on a Wednesday. She's just gotten off a tense call with a client who keeps moving the goalposts on a logo project, asking for "just one more round of revisions" for the fourth time. She feels that familiar knot in her stomach—frustration mixed with the creeping fear that maybe she's not good enough, maybe she should've pushed back harder, maybe she's being taken advantage of.

The email subject line: "Extra 30% off sale items—today only."

She clicks.

Here's what you need to understand: Sarah doesn't *decide* to start shopping. She doesn't think, "I'm feeling stressed, so I'll go buy clothes to feel better." The click is almost automatic. Her finger moves before her conscious mind even registers the choice.

That click—that's the **cue** responding to the trigger. The trigger is external: the email, the subject line, the promise of a deal. But the cue is internal: the feeling of stress, inadequacy, the desire for control over *something* in a day that feels chaotic.

Within seconds, she's scrolling. Midi dress in rust. Linen blazer. High-waisted jeans she definitely doesn't need because she already has three pairs in her closet that she rotates through.

But that's not what her brain is seeing.

Her brain is painting a picture of what owning these things will *feel* like. She imagines herself in that rust dress on a video call, looking effortlessly professional. She imagines the client being impressed, saying yes to the proposal without pushback. She imagines feeling confident, capable, like the kind of person who doesn't get walked over.

That's the **craving**. It's not about the dress. It never is.

The craving is for relief—from stress, from inadequacy, from the uncomfortable knot in her stomach that's been sitting there since the client call ended. And her brain has learned, through hundreds of previous iterations of this exact loop, that buying something delivers that relief. Fast.

She adds the dress to her cart. Then the blazer. Then, what the hell, the jeans too. She's already at $180. If she hits $200, shipping is free.

She finds a $22 T-shirt.

Checkout is three clicks. Saved payment info. Saved address. Confirm.

That's the **response**—the compulsive action. It happens with minimal conscious thought. It feels less like a decision and more like momentum, like she's sliding downhill and her body is just following the path of least resistance.

And for exactly twelve seconds, she feels *good*.

There's a little buzz of satisfaction. Dopamine, lighting up her reward centers. Her brain registers this as: *Problem solved. Threat neutralized. You're okay now.*

She closes the browser. Goes back to work on the logo revisions. The knot in her stomach has loosened.

But here's the thing about that relief: it doesn't last.

By the next morning, the dress is already less appealing. She's lying in bed, scrolling through her bank app, and sees the charge: $202.47. She thinks about the credit card bill due in two weeks. She thinks about the fact that she's supposed to be saving for a trip to visit her sister, and she just blew $200 on clothes she doesn't need.

The relief has curdled into guilt.

And that guilt? That's not the end of the loop. That's *fuel* for the next one.

Because now she has a new uncomfortable feeling to escape from. Disappointment in herself. Frustration that she did it again. And what's one way her brain has learned to temporarily fix uncomfortable feelings?

You see where this is going.

That's the loop: **Cue -> Craving -> Response -> Relief -> Regret -> Repeat.**

It's not a moral failing. It's not weakness. It's your brain doing exactly what it evolved to do: seeking pleasure, avoiding pain, learning patterns that deliver rewards.

The problem is that the reward is a lie.

Or at least, it's temporary enough that it might as well be. That dopamine hit Sarah gets when she clicks "Complete Purchase"? It's real. It's measurable. If you stuck her in an fMRI machine, you'd see her nucleus accumbens light up like a Christmas tree.

But dopamine isn't released when you *get* the reward. It's released in *anticipation* of it.

Think about waiting for food at a restaurant. You've ordered your favorite dish. You can smell it being prepared. You're imagining that first bite. That flutter of excitement, that almost-nervous energy? That's dopamine. It's building as you get closer to the thing you want.

For impulse shoppers, this system gets hijacked.

The reward isn't the dress showing up on Sarah's doorstep three days later. The reward is the *idea* of the dress. The imagined confidence boost. The fantasy version of herself who wears it to client calls and feels effortlessly capable.

Her brain starts releasing dopamine at the mere *thought* of acquiring it. And that creates the craving—this intense, almost physical *wanting* that overrides rational thought.

This is why browsing online stores feels so compelling even when you don't intend to buy anything. Each scroll reveals potential rewards. A cute top. A discounted gadget. A book you might enjoy. Each item delivers a tiny dose of dopamine. You're not shopping for things; you're shopping for the *feeling* of possibility.

It's the same mechanism that makes slot machines so addictive. The intermittent reward schedule—you never know when the next win will come—keeps you hooked. One more spin. One more scroll. One more page.

And here's where it gets worse: stress amplifies this effect.

When you're stressed, anxious, or feeling low, your baseline dopamine levels drop. Your brain goes into seek mode, actively hunting for things that can boost them back up. And impulsive purchases—fast, easy, reliable—are one of the quickest fixes available.

Sarah's impulse buys always spiked when work got chaotic. It wasn't a coincidence. She was self-medicating with shopping, using it as an emotional regulation tool. Except it's a tool that costs money, creates debt, and ultimately makes the underlying stress worse.

You know what's even more insidious? The guilt and regret *after* the purchase don't break the cycle. They feed it.

Because now Sarah doesn't just have the original stress from the difficult client. She also has the disappointment of having spent money she didn't want to spend. She has the shame of doing it *again*, even though she told herself last time would be the last time.

And what does her brain do with those feelings?

It goes looking for another dopamine hit.

Let me be clear about what this costs.

I'm not talking about the $202 Sarah spent on that one purchase. I'm talking about what happens when you run this loop on repeat for months. Years.

Let's do the math, because I think you need to see it written out.

Sarah averages two impulse clothing purchases a week. Sometimes it's one big order; sometimes it's a couple smaller ones. But it averages out to about $180 a week. That's $720 a month. $8,640 a year.

In five years, that's $43,200.

Forty-three thousand dollars. Gone. Not invested. Not saved. Not spent on things she genuinely values—travel, or experiences with friends, or even high-quality pieces she'd actually wear regularly.

Spent on clothes that mostly sit in her closet with the tags still on.

But the financial cost isn't even the worst part.

The worst part is the weight of it. The mental load of knowing you're doing something that doesn't serve you and feeling powerless to stop. The shame spiral of promising yourself you'll do better, then breaking that promise three days later when another sale email hits your inbox.

Sarah described it to me once as "failing a test I didn't study for, over and over, every single week." That low-grade sense of defeat that colors everything else.

It makes the good things in her life harder to enjoy. She'll be out to dinner with friends, and in the back of her mind, she's thinking about the credit card balance. She'll see something she actually *wants*—a weekend trip, a concert ticket—and she'll hesitate, because she's already spent so much on things she didn't even want that much.

The impulse loop doesn't just drain your bank account. It drains your sense of agency.

It makes you feel like you're not in control of your own choices. Like some other version of you—impulsive, short-sighted, weak—keeps taking over and making decisions that the real you has to clean up later.

And here's the thing I wish someone had told me earlier, back when I was buying my third meal-planning app of the month: *that feeling of being out of control is the whole point.*

Not in some conspiracy theory way. But the entire infrastructure of online shopping is designed to make the impulse loop as frictionless as possible.

One-click ordering. Saved payment info. "Buy Now" buttons in Instagram ads that let you check out without ever leaving the app. Email subject lines optimized through A/B testing to trigger FOMO. Countdown timers. "Only 3 left in stock!" warnings.

Every single piece of that system is engineered to reduce the gap between craving and response. To make the action so fast, so automatic, that your rational brain doesn't have time to catch up.

You're not failing a willpower test. You're trying to resist a system that's been optimized by millions of dollars in research and development to bypass your willpower entirely.

So no, trying harder isn't the answer.

Understanding the loop is.

Here's what Sarah did.

First, she stopped trying to fight the cravings head-on. That was the old strategy—white-knuckling it, telling herself "just don't click," relying on discipline alone. It worked sometimes. But it failed often enough that she'd end up right back in the loop, feeling worse for having "failed."

Instead, she started interrupting the loop at a different point.

Not at the craving. At the response.

When she felt the urge to shop—and she *would* feel it; that wasn't going away—she didn't try to suppress it. She acknowledged it. Then she built in friction between the craving and the action.

Here's the system she used. I call it **Cue, Pause, Redirect.**

Cue: Notice the moment the urge appears. For Sarah, it was usually a physical sensation—tightness in her chest, restlessness, the impulse to open a shopping site. Sometimes it followed a specific trigger (sale email, Instagram ad). Sometimes it just emerged from a vague feeling of stress or boredom.

The key was noticing it *as it happened*, not ten minutes later after she'd already added three things to her cart.

Pause: This is the friction. The moment she noticed the urge, she set a timer for 15 minutes. Not an hour. Not tomorrow. Fifteen minutes.

During those 15 minutes, the rule was: she couldn't shop. That's it. She wasn't banning herself from buying. She was just delaying the action.

Redirect: While the timer ran, she did something else. Anything else. She'd sketch something in her notebook. Text a friend. Go outside and walk around the block. Watch a YouTube video about design trends.

The activity didn't matter. What mattered was breaking the momentum between craving and response.

Here's what happened in practice:

Sarah would be at her desk, feeling that familiar pull to check if Everlane had added anything new to their sale section. She'd notice it—that's the cue. She'd set her phone timer for 15 minutes and open her sketchbook instead. She'd start drawing. Nothing fancy. Usually just shapes, patterns, little visual ideas.

By the time the timer went off, one of two things had happened.

Either the urge had faded—not disappeared, but dulled enough that she could look at it clearly and decide it wasn't worth acting on. Or it was still there, and she'd ask herself one question: *What am I actually trying to fix right now?*

Sometimes the answer was “I’m stressed about the client call.” Sometimes it was “I’m bored.” Sometimes it was “I feel like I don’t have anything nice.”

And once she had that answer, she could address the actual problem instead of medicating it with a purchase.

Stressed? She’d take a real break—go for a walk, call a friend, work on a personal project that reminded her why she liked design in the first place.

Bored? She’d find something engaging that didn’t involve spending money.

Feeling like she didn’t have anything nice? That one was trickier, because it usually pointed to a deeper issue—comparing herself to other designers, feeling like she wasn’t measuring up. But at least she could *see* it for what it was, instead of covering it up with another dress she wouldn’t wear.

The pause didn’t eliminate impulse spending overnight. Sarah still bought things. But the frequency dropped. And more importantly, the *feeling* around it changed.

She wasn’t failing a test anymore. She was running an experiment. Gathering data. Learning which cues were strongest, which redirects worked best, which underlying feelings she needed to address in other ways.

Within two months, her average weekly spending on clothes dropped from $180 to around $40. Not zero—she still liked clothes, still bought things she genuinely wanted. But the compulsive, regret-laden purchases almost disappeared.

The money was great. The sense of control was better.

You're probably thinking: *Okay, but 15 minutes isn't enough. The urge will still be there.*

And you're right. Sometimes it is.

But here's what you're missing: the urge doesn't need to disappear. It just needs to weaken enough that your rational brain can step in and evaluate whether acting on it serves you.

The impulse loop thrives on speed. The faster you move from craving to response, the less time your prefrontal cortex—the part of your brain responsible for planning, decision-making, moderating social behavior—has to weigh in.

That's why one-click ordering is so effective. It compresses the timeline. By the time your rational brain says "Wait, do I actually want this?", the order's already placed.

The pause expands the timeline. It gives your rational brain a chance to catch up.

Think of it like this: your emotional brain is a toddler. Fast, impulsive, operates on *I want it NOW*. Your rational brain is the parent. Slower, more deliberative, thinks about consequences.

When the toddler wants candy at the grocery store checkout, the parent doesn't say "You can never have candy." That just leads to a tantrum. The parent says, "Not right now. We'll talk about it when we get home."

By the time you get home, the toddler might still want the candy. But the intensity has faded. You can have a conversation about it. Maybe the toddler gets a small piece. Maybe they get distracted by something else. Maybe they realize they're not actually that hungry.

The pause is you parenting your own impulses.

And before you roll your eyes at the idea of treating yourself like a toddler, let me tell you: your impulses *are* toddler-like. That's not an insult. That's neuroscience.

The limbic system—the part of your brain that generates cravings, emotions, impulses—is ancient. It evolved millions of years ago, long before humans developed language or abstract reasoning. It's fast, powerful, and operates on simple rules: *This feels good. Do it again.*

The prefrontal cortex—your rational brain—is newer. And it's slower. It takes time to process information, weigh options, consider long-term consequences.

When you're tired, stressed, or distracted, the prefrontal cortex goes offline even more. That's why impulse spending spikes late at night, after a hard day, when your rational defenses are worn down.

The pause gives your prefrontal cortex time to boot back up.

Let me show you another version of this.

Mark is a 34-year-old software developer in Austin. Works remotely. Makes good money. And keeps buying tech gadgets he doesn't need.

New mechanical keyboards. Monitor arms. Standing desk converters. Webcam upgrades. Software subscriptions that promise to optimize his workflow, make him more productive, help him finally become the kind of developer who ships side projects instead of just thinking about them.

His home office is a graveyard of abandoned optimizations.

The pattern started innocently enough. He wanted to improve his workspace. He'd read articles about ergonomics, watch YouTube videos about developer setups, scroll through Reddit threads where people shared photos of their minimalist desks with perfectly cable-managed everything.

And he'd feel that familiar pang: inadequacy mixed with hope.

If I just had that setup, I'd be more focused. More productive. I'd finally finish that app idea I've been sitting on.

The trigger for Mark wasn't sale emails. It was comparison. Seeing what other developers had—or at least, what they *showed* having—and feeling like he was behind.

The craving was for capability. For the feeling of being the kind of person who had his shit together.

The response was ordering another piece of equipment.

The relief was imagining himself using it, finally being productive, finally shipping something.

The regret came a week later when the new keyboard sat on his desk, used once, while he went back to his old one because the key switches were too loud for video calls.

By the time Mark contacted me, he'd spent over $4,000 in a single year on workspace upgrades. And his productivity hadn't changed at all.

Because the problem was never his equipment. The problem was that he was trying to buy confidence.

Here's what he did to break the loop.

He started tracking triggers. Every time he felt the urge to buy something, he wrote down what happened right before. What was he doing? What was he feeling?

The pattern became obvious fast: he'd spend an hour scrolling through tech YouTube or Reddit, see someone's impressive setup, and immediately feel like his own workspace was inadequate. Within minutes, he'd have five tabs open comparing prices on ultrawide monitors.

So he added friction at the trigger level, not just the response level.

He unsubscribed from tech YouTube channels that focused on gear. He filtered out the setup-photo subreddits. He stopped following developers who constantly posted about their equipment.

And when he *did* feel the urge to buy something—because cutting out triggers doesn't eliminate cravings entirely—he used a variation of Sarah's system.

Fifteen-minute timer. During that time, he'd work on his side project. Actually write code. Actually make progress on the thing he kept telling himself he needed better equipment to do.

Funny thing: he started shipping.

Not because he finally had the right keyboard or the perfect monitor setup. Because he stopped spending his energy shopping for solutions and started actually working.

Within four months, he launched a small app. Nothing huge—a habit tracker he built for himself that a few other people found useful. But it was *done*. Out in the world.

He told me later that finishing that project did more for his sense of capability than any piece of equipment ever had.

And his impulse tech purchases dropped by about 80%. He still upgraded things occasionally. But it was intentional. Based on actual needs, not imagined ones.

Here's what both Sarah and Mark figured out, and what I want you to understand:

The impulse loop isn't something you conquer once and move on from.

It's something you manage. Ongoing. Like brushing your teeth or doing laundry.

You don't brush your teeth once and declare victory over cavities forever. You build a routine. You do it every day. Some days you're more thorough than others. Some days you forget. But the habit, over time, is what keeps your teeth from falling out.

The impulse loop is the same.

You're not aiming for perfection. You're aiming for a system that makes the loop less automatic, less destructive, more something you can observe and choose whether to engage with.

Some days you'll notice the cue, pause, redirect, and the urge will fade. Some days you'll still buy the thing. Some days you'll buy the thing and feel fine about it because it was actually worth it.

The goal isn't to never spend money impulsively again. The goal is to stop spending money *compulsively*—on autopilot, driven by emotions you're not even aware of, in ways that don't align with what you actually value.

And the way you do that isn't by trying harder.

It's by understanding the loop. By seeing it clearly enough to interrupt it. By building friction into the system so your rational brain has time to catch up with your impulses.

You don't need more discipline. You need better design.

So here's where we go next: if the impulse loop thrives on speed and frictionlessness, the solution is to slow it down. To add obstacles—not giant walls you have to scale, but small speed bumps that give you a chance to think before you act. In the next chapter, we're going to talk about friction as a tool. How to build it into your spending systems. How to make the impulse purchases just hard enough that your rational brain has time to ask whether this is really what you want. Because once you see how powerful friction can be, you'll stop thinking of obstacles as annoyances and start seeing them as one of the most effective tools you have.

But before we get there, there's one more piece of the impulse loop worth understanding: the story you tell yourself afterward.

Because here's what happens after you've made the purchase. You're holding the package, or the notification has arrived, or you're looking at the thing you just bought—and there's this brief window where your brain tries to make sense of what just happened. And what it usually does is construct a narrative that makes the purchase feel reasonable. Even inevitable.

"I deserved this." "I've been working so hard." "It was on sale—I actually saved money." "I'll use it all the time." "This is an investment in myself."

None of these are lies, exactly. But they're not the whole truth either. They're the story your brain tells to smooth over the gap between what you intended to do with your money and what you actually did. Psychologists call this post-purchase rationalization, and it's one of the most insidious parts of the loop because it prevents you from learning. If every impulse purchase gets reframed as a smart decision, you never build the pattern recognition that would help you spot the next one coming.

And this is where a lot of people get stuck. They know they're spending too much. They feel guilty about it. But they can't quite connect the dots between the individual purchases—each of which felt justified in the moment—and the larger pattern that's draining their accounts. The rationalization story is so good, so immediate, that it overwrites the data before you can see it clearly.

This is why tracking your spending often fails. You look at the list of transactions and each one has a story attached. The coffee was because you were exhausted. The book was research. The shoes were a replacement for the ones that wore out. Taken individually, they all make sense. It's only when you zoom out and see the frequency, the volume, the sheer accumulated weight of all those reasonable-sounding decisions that the pattern becomes visible.

But even then, even when you see it, there's a deeper loop at work. Because the impulse loop isn't just about acquiring things. It's about how you feel about yourself.

Think about the moment right before you buy something on impulse. What's the emotional state? For a lot of people, it's not happiness. It's something closer to restlessness. Boredom. A vague sense of lack. Maybe you're procrastinating on something that feels hard. Maybe you're avoiding a conversation you don't want to have. Maybe you just feel... off, and you don't know why.

The purchase offers a solution. It's a hit of novelty, of possibility, of control. For a few minutes, you're not the person who's behind on their goals or anxious about money or unsure about the future. You're someone making a decision, taking action, acquiring something new. It feels like progress.

And that feeling is real. The problem is that it doesn't last. The package arrives, or the digital download completes, or the transaction goes through—and within hours, sometimes minutes, you're back to baseline. The restlessness returns. The sense of lack creeps back in. And because the loop has been reinforced, your brain has learned that spending is a reliable way to feel better, even if the relief is temporary.

This is the part most people don't talk about when they talk about impulse spending. It's not really about the stuff. It's about the emotional regulation. The spending is a coping mechanism, and like all coping mechanisms, it works just well enough to keep you coming back, but not well enough to actually solve the underlying problem.

Which means that if you try to stop the spending without addressing the emotions driving it, you're going to struggle. You'll feel deprived. You'll feel like you're denying yourself something you need. Because in a very real sense, you are—you're cutting off a strategy your brain has come to rely on for managing discomfort.

This is why willpower fails. This is why you can be fully committed in the morning and completely derailed by the afternoon. You're not weak. You're just trying to use conscious restraint to override a system that operates below the level of conscious thought. It's like trying to hold your breath indefinitely. You can do it for a while, but eventually your body overrides the decision and makes you breathe.

So what's the alternative? If willpower doesn't work, and awareness alone isn't enough, what do you do?

You change the environment. You redesign the systems. You stop trying to be strong enough to resist every individual temptation and start building a life where the temptations are fewer, quieter, and easier to ignore. You don't fight the impulse loop head-on. You dismantle it, piece by piece, until the path of least resistance is also the path that aligns with what you actually want.

And that's where friction comes in.

MealFlow Premium is still on my phone. I paid $4.99 for it three years ago. It's sent 1,847 notifications I've ignored. I keep meaning to delete it.

I closed my laptop, walked to my car, and checked my phone. MealFlow Premium had already sent its first notification: 'Plan your week!' I swiped it away and drove home to a kitchen I'd already rigged against me without realizing it.

Chapter 3: Friction as a Force Multiplier

Amazon's 'Buy Now with 1-Click' button was patented in 1997 and has generated billions in impulse purchases. Deleting your Amazon account in 2024 takes seven confirmation screens, two security checks, and a cooling-off period. The asymmetry isn't an accident.

I was trying to delete my Amazon account. Not pause it. Not "take a break." Actually delete it. Gone forever. The nuclear option.

I'd woken up that morning to three shipping confirmations for things I'd bought the night before while scrolling in bed: a sous vide machine I had zero intention of learning to use, a book about productivity that would join the stack of unread productivity books on my nightstand, and—this was the one that broke me—a phone stand that cost forty-two dollars. My phone case cost fifteen.

You know what Amazon made me do? Click through seven separate "Are you sure?" screens. Each one designed differently. Each one with a new argument for why leaving would be a terrible mistake. By screen four, they were showing me a highlight reel of my past purchases, like some kind of shopping nostalgia trip. *Remember when you bought this spatula? Good times, right? You sure you want to throw that relationship away?*

I gave up. Closed the tab. The account stayed open.

Here's what got me: Amazon will build a seven-layer fortress to keep you from leaving, but buying something? Three seconds. One click. Your card's saved. Your address is saved. Your impulse control? Not even part of the equation.

That's not an accident. That's design. And if a trillion-dollar company understands that friction shapes behavior, maybe we should pay attention.

The thing is, you already know this. Not intellectually—you *feel* it. You've felt it every time you bought something at 11 PM that you didn't need, didn't really want, and definitely shouldn't have spent money on. That specific sinking sensation when the package arrives and you can barely remember ordering it.

But knowing doesn't stop it from happening. That's the cruel part.

I need to tell you about Sarah, because her story is the one that made me understand what the absence of friction actually costs. And it's not just money, though that's part of it.

Sarah teaches fifth grade in Austin. Makes decent money—not wealthy, but comfortable enough that $250 a month shouldn't have felt catastrophic. Except it did. Every month, like clockwork, $250 disappeared into what she called her "scroll hole."

Late-night purchases, mostly. She'd be in bed, phone in hand, and the algorithm would start showing her things. A ceramic planter shaped like a sleeping cat—$38. That one arrived and sat empty on her kitchen counter for four months before she finally bought a plant for it. A linen dress in a color she'd never actually wear—$76. Still in her closet with the tags on. Hand-poured candles that cost sixty dollars and smelled, as she put it, "like a hotel lobby I'm never going to stay in." One was labeled "Woodland Berry." It smelled like neither woodland nor berry. It smelled like someone's idea of what rich people's bathrooms should smell like.

She didn't need any of it. The knowing part was never the problem.

Let me tell you what it cost her, though, because this is the part that matters and the part we usually skip over when we talk about impulse spending like it's just a financial mistake you fix with better budgeting.

It wasn't just the money—though $250 a month is $3,000 a year, which is a decent vacation or a substantial emergency fund or about a million other things that might have actually improved her life. It was the *feeling*. Every single time Sarah saw a shipping confirmation email, she felt a little wave of shame. Not dramatic, not life-ruining. Just this low-level "why did I do that again" feeling that she'd carry around for a few hours. Sometimes a few days.

Add that up over a year. Dozens of small shame spirals. Dozens of moments of looking at something she'd bought and thinking, "What was I thinking?" Dozens of times hiding packages from her roommate because she didn't want to explain another delivery. Her roommate wasn't judgmental—Sarah was. She'd imagine the conversation: *Another package? What is it this time?* And she'd take the box straight to her room without opening it in the common areas.

The financial cost was real. The emotional cost was worse. Here's the thing that really got to her, the thing she told me over coffee when we first talked about this: she *knew it was happening* and she still couldn't stop it.

She'd read all the articles about mindful spending and dopamine hits and how Instagram is basically designed to make you feel inadequate enough to buy things. She could explain the psychology of impulse purchases better than I can. She once gave me a whole breakdown of the sunk-cost fallacy and how it applies to online shopping carts—how keeping items in your cart makes you feel like you've already invested in them, so removing them feels like a loss.

Knowing is supposed to help, right? Understanding the mechanism should give you power over it.

Didn't work. Not even close.

That feeling—that you're smarter than this but somehow that doesn't matter, that knowing better doesn't mean doing better—that's what the absence of friction costs you. Not just money. The feeling that you're not in control of your own decisions.

Sarah tried the classic advice. "Just don't buy it." Lasted about nine hours. She tried budgeting apps—seven of them, actually, before she gave up. Most of them were designed by people who don't actually struggle with impulse spending, so they assumed the problem was not knowing where your money went. Sarah knew exactly where her money went. That wasn't the issue. She tried writing herself notes—"Do I really need this?" stuck to her phone case. She tried promising herself she'd do better. She tried everything except the one thing that actually works.

Making it harder.

Friction isn't about willpower. It's about design. Right now, your financial life is designed to make spending effortless and saving hard. That's not a moral failing on your part—that's billions of dollars of research and optimization working against you.

Every company with a website has poured money into making buying as seamless as possible. One-click checkout. Saved payment methods. “Buy now, pay later” options that let you skip the part where you actually reckon with whether you can afford something. Algorithms that show you exactly what you want before you know you want it.

Amazon didn’t patent one-click ordering as a courtesy to busy customers. They did it because removing friction increases sales.

There’s a whole field of research around this—e-commerce conversion optimization, they call it—and the core finding is dead simple: every extra step you add to checkout costs you customers. One additional form field can drop conversion rates by double digits. Making someone re-enter their credit card information? That’s a barrier a lot of potential buyers won’t cross.

Businesses know this. They spend fortunes removing every possible obstacle between “I want that” and “I own that.” The path is a water slide. Smooth, fast, designed to keep you moving in one direction.

So why not build the opposite? Why not add speed bumps?

I know what you’re thinking. You’re thinking this sounds inconvenient. And yeah, it is. But inconvenient is the whole point, and if you can stay with me for a minute I’ll show you why inconvenience might be the most valuable thing you can build into your financial life.

Sarah started with payment information. She deleted all of it. Every shopping app on her phone, every website she’d ever bought from. Instagram shopping, Etsy, Target, that boutique site that kept sending her emails about sustainable loungewear. If she wanted to buy something, she had to get up, find her purse, pull out her credit card, and manually type in sixteen digits plus the expiration date and security code.

It sounds almost stupid when you say it out loud. What's ninety seconds of typing? How is that going to stop anything?

Those ninety seconds were enough to disrupt the impulse. Not every time—she still bought things—but often enough that her spending dropped by half in the first month.

Here's what happened in those ninety seconds: her brain woke up.

The automatic behavior got interrupted. She had to make an actual decision instead of just following the frictionless path from wanting to having.

Sometimes she still decided to buy the thing. That's fine. The point isn't to never spend money—it's to spend money on purpose instead of on autopilot.

But Sarah didn't stop there. She added a second layer: the "want" list. Anything that made her reach for her wallet had to go on the list first. The item, the price, where she saw it. And then—this is the part that actually mattered—she couldn't buy it for 48 hours.

That waiting period changed everything.

About 70% of the things on her list never got purchased. The ceramic cat planter that seemed essential at 11 PM looked kind of ridiculous two days later in the actual light of day. The linen dress stopped making sense when she thought about where she'd actually wear it. The urgency faded. The dopamine wore off. What remained was a more honest assessment of whether she actually wanted to exchange her money for that object.

For the things that survived the waiting period—the other 30%—Sarah added one more step. She had to calculate how many hours of teaching it would cost her. That $75 sweater? Two and a half hours in a classroom. Two and a half hours of explaining fractions and mediating arguments about who gets to be line leader and reminding kids that yes, they do need to show their work even if they got the right answer.

When you frame it that way, the sweater feels different.

It's not just $75 anymore. It's 150 minutes of your actual life, translated into money, translated into an object you'll wear maybe a dozen times.

Sometimes that equation still made sense. Sometimes Sarah decided the sweater was worth it. But most of the time? It wasn't.

Let me tell you what happened to me, because I want you to see that this isn't some abstract system I'm prescribing from a distance. I had to figure this out for myself, and I got it wrong several times before I got it right.

My particular weakness wasn't clothes or home goods. It was books. Which sounds almost noble, right? At least it's *books*. At least you're feeding your mind, investing in yourself, all those things we tell ourselves when we want to justify spending money on something.

Except I wasn't reading them.

I was buying them because buying them *felt* like self-improvement. It felt productive. Like I was investing in my future self—the version of me who had time to read, who would definitely get around to all these fascinating topics. But the stack of unread books on my nightstand kept growing, and my bank account kept shrinking, and one day I counted twelve books I'd bought in the last two months that I hadn't even opened. Some of them I'd forgotten I owned.

There was a book on behavioral economics. A memoir by someone I'd never heard of but whose interview I'd enjoyed on a podcast. Two books on writing—I'm a writer, I told myself, this is professional development. A book about the history of salt. I don't even remember why I bought that one. It's still on my shelf, unopened. The Salt Book, we call it now. A monument to purchases made at 11 PM.

So I made a rule. Deleted my card from every online bookstore. If I wanted to buy a book, I had to go to an actual physical bookstore. In person. With cash.

Do you know how long it had been since I'd been inside a bookstore? Months. Maybe longer. Buying books online was so easy I'd forgotten bookstores existed. Click, click, done. The book arrives in two days. The hit of accomplishment arrives immediately, which is really what I was buying—not the book itself, but the feeling of having made a good choice.

The rule cut my book-buying by about 80%. Not because I stopped wanting books. I still wanted them. But wanting them wasn't enough anymore. I had to want them enough to get in my car, drive somewhere, find parking, walk inside, browse, stand in line, hand over actual physical money.

Most of the time, the desire wasn't strong enough to survive all those steps.

The books I did buy? I read them. Because I'd invested effort in acquiring them. They weren't just another dopamine hit from a late-night click. They were books I'd chosen deliberately, that I'd physically gone out and gotten. That changes the relationship.

Let me give you a framework. Not because I think frameworks are magical—most of the time they're just a way to organize what you already know—but because structure helps when you're trying to change behavior you've been running on autopilot for years.

Layer One: Remove Easy Access

This is the obvious step, and most people skip it because it feels inconvenient. Which—and I really cannot stress this enough—is the entire point.

Delete your saved payment information. All of it. Every shopping site, every app, every saved card in your phone's autofill. Make yourself enter it manually every single time.

I'm serious about this. Not "delete most of them." All of them. Because the ones you keep are going to be the ones you use. If you leave Amazon saved because "I actually need things from Amazon sometimes," then Amazon is going to be where your impulse spending lives. Delete it anyway. If you actually need something from Amazon, you can re-enter your card. It's not that hard. It just makes you stop and think first.

Unsubscribe from promotional emails. Not just the ones from stores you don't shop at—*especially* the ones from stores you do. Those emails exist for one reason: to create desire where none existed before. You weren't thinking about needing new jeans until you got that email about 40% off denim. Now you're thinking about it. Now you're clicking through. Now you're buying jeans you don't need because they're "on sale."

Here's something nobody tells you: "on sale" is not the same as "a good deal." A good deal is when you need something, you were going to buy it anyway, and you happened to find it for less. "On sale" is when you buy something you don't need because the discount makes you feel smart. You're not saving money. You're spending money you wouldn't have spent otherwise. The discount is bait.

If you're serious about this, delete the apps entirely. Or at least move them into a folder that's not on your home screen. Make yourself swipe, search, find. Add fifteen seconds of friction between the impulse and the action.

This layer won't stop you from spending if you really want something. If you're determined, you'll re-enter your credit card. You'll re-download the app. But it disrupts the automatic behavior. It makes you choose the path instead of just falling into it.

Layer Two: Implement a Waiting Period

This is where you build in time for your rational brain to catch up with your emotional impulses.

The standard version is 24 hours. I recommend 48. Longer is better, to a point—if you make it a full week, you might forget about the item entirely, which sort of defeats the purpose. You want to remember it and reconsider it, not just lose track of it.

Here's how it works: when you see something you want, you don't buy it. You add it to a list. Notes app on your phone, a bookmark folder, a physical notebook, whatever. Write down what it is, how much it costs, where you saw it. Then walk away.

You cannot buy the item until the waiting period is over. This is non-negotiable.

No exceptions for small purchases—those add up faster than the big ones. No exceptions for sales or "limited time offers"—there is always another sale. I promise you, the thing you want will either still be available in 48 hours, or something similar will be. And if it's not? If it sells out and you never get it? That's fine. There will be other things. The scarcity is artificial. They make you feel like you're missing out so you'll act fast. Don't fall for it.

After the waiting period, look at the list again. A lot of the items won't seem as appealing anymore. The urgency will have faded. You might not even remember why you wanted it. If that's the case, delete it and move on.

If you still want it after 48 hours, you might actually want it. But before you buy it, move to layer three.

Layer Three: Add a Small, Annoying Task

This is the layer most people skip, and it's the one that actually makes the system stick.

Even after the waiting period, you're not allowed to just buy the thing. You have to complete one additional task first. Something mildly annoying. Not punitive—this isn't about punishing yourself for wanting things—but annoying enough that it forces you to consider whether the purchase is really worth the effort.

Options:

- Text a friend and ask their honest opinion about whether you should buy it. Not a friend who's going to just tell you what you want to hear. A friend who'll actually ask why you want it. - Calculate how many hours of work it would take to pay for it. After taxes. Be honest about your actual hourly rate. - Go for a 20-minute walk before making the purchase. No phone. Just walk. - Write out, by hand, three reasons you want it and three reasons you don't need it. See which list is more convincing.

The task itself doesn't matter that much. What matters is that it adds another layer of deliberate decision-making. It gives you one more chance to stop and ask: is this really what I want to do with my money?

David's situation was different, and it shows you can adapt this however you need to.

David's a freelance photographer. Early forties, lives in Portland, shoots weddings and corporate events. Makes decent money—not rich, but solid. His impulse-spending problem? Camera gear.

Lenses, mostly. Also tripods, memory cards, lighting equipment, anything that could remotely be justified as a "business expense" even though he already owned everything he actually needed to do his job. He had lenses he'd used exactly once. A tripod still in the box. Memory cards he bought because they were faster, even though his old ones worked fine.

The thing is, David's spending wasn't emotional. He wasn't buying lenses because he was stressed or bored or trying to fill some void. He was buying them because he's a gear nerd. He loved the research. Reading reviews, watching YouTube comparisons, diving into specs. The research itself was enjoyable. And once he'd spent three hours researching a lens, buying it felt like the natural conclusion. He'd already invested the time. Might as well complete the process.

For David, a simple waiting period didn't work. He could easily spend 48 hours researching a lens, and by the end of it he'd be even more convinced he needed it. He could explain to you, in great detail, why this particular lens was going to transform his work. The research didn't cool his desire—it amplified it.

So we added different friction.

Before he could even consider buying any piece of gear over $200, he had to spend two hours editing photos from a recent shoot using only the equipment he already owned. Not researching new gear. Not browsing reviews. Actually using what he had.

This did two things.

First, it reminded him he already owned excellent equipment. He didn't need the newest lens to take great photos—he was already taking great photos. His clients weren't complaining. His portfolio wasn't suffering. The limitation wasn't the gear. It never is, really, but when you're deep in research mode it's easy to convince yourself that the thing standing between you and better work is the thing you don't own yet.

Second, it forced him to focus on the creative process instead of the acquisition process. It reminded him why he became a photographer in the first place. Not to collect gear. To make images.

After implementing that rule, David's gear spending dropped from around $400 a month to maybe $50. He still bought things occasionally—there were purchases that genuinely made sense for his work. But the constant low-level acquisition stopped.

The key was tailoring the friction to his specific trigger. Sarah's trigger was emotional—late-night scrolling, stress relief—so her friction needed to disrupt the impulse quickly. David's trigger was intellectual. He enjoyed the research phase. So his friction needed to redirect his focus back to actually using what he already owned.

Your trigger is probably different from both of theirs. That's fine. The framework is the same: identify when and why you spend impulsively, then design friction that specifically disrupts that pattern.

I know what you're about to say. "Okay, but what if I actually need something quickly? What if there's a real sale, or an emergency, or a legitimate reason to buy something right away?"

Fair question. The answer is: you build in exceptions, but you make them explicit and narrow.

Sarah's system had one exception: anything under ten dollars didn't require the waiting period. She could buy a coffee or a sandwich or a phone charger without going through the whole process. That kept the system from feeling oppressive. She wasn't trying to control every single dollar—she was trying to stop the $40 planters and $75 dresses that added up to real money.

David's system had a different exception: if a piece of equipment broke and he had a paying job coming up that required it, he could buy a replacement immediately. But—and this was important—it had to be a replacement, not an upgrade. If his 50mm lens broke, he could buy another 50mm. He couldn't use it as an excuse to finally get that 85mm he'd been eyeing.

The point of exceptions isn't to give yourself an easy out. It's to keep the system realistic and sustainable. If your friction system is so rigid that you violate it constantly, it's not working. Better to have a few well-defined exceptions you actually follow than a perfect system you abandon after a week.

My exception is gifts. If I'm buying something for someone else, I don't make myself wait 48 hours or go to a physical store. Partly because gifts are different—I'm not buying them for the dopamine hit, I'm buying them because I want to give someone something they'll enjoy. But also, practically speaking, if I'm shopping for a birthday or holiday, I probably have a deadline. The waiting period doesn't help. It just adds stress.

But here's the thing: I don't let myself use "gift" as a loophole. If I'm buying something that's primarily for me but I'm telling myself it's for someone else—like buying a book I want to read and planning to give it to a friend after I'm done—that's not a gift. That's me gaming my own system. It goes on the wait list.

You have to be honest with yourself about what counts as an exception and what's just you trying to avoid the friction. The system only works if you actually follow it.

Here's the part where I'm supposed to give you a step-by-step implementation guide, right? Five numbered action items with deadlines and accountability metrics?

I'm not going to do that.

Because if you're reading this chapter, you already know what you need to do. You don't need me to tell you to delete your saved credit cards or start a want list. You need permission to make your life slightly more inconvenient in service of a larger goal.

So here's your permission: it's okay to make things harder for yourself. It's okay to add steps between wanting something and getting it. It's okay to slow down in a world that's constantly trying to speed you up.

Start with one thing. Just one. Pick the friction layer that feels most manageable.

Maybe it's deleting saved payment info. Start there. Spend an evening going through every app and website where your card is saved and remove it. Yes, it's tedious. Yes, you'll be tempted to leave a few "just in case." Don't. Delete all of them. You can always re-enter the information later if you actually need it.

Maybe it's starting a 24-hour waiting period. Get a notebook or open a note on your phone and start writing down things you want instead of buying them immediately. Set a timer on your phone for 24 hours from when you add each item. When the timer goes off, look at the item again. Still want it? Move it to the 48-hour list. Don't want it anymore? Delete it and feel the small victory of money you didn't spend.

Maybe it's something I haven't mentioned because I don't know your specific situation. Maybe you need to unfollow all the Instagram accounts that make you feel like you need new clothes. Maybe you need to change your route home from work so you don't pass the store that always pulls you in. Maybe you need to delete your

Amazon app and only let yourself order from a desktop computer, which you don't have in bed at 11 PM.

The specific action doesn't matter as much as the principle: you're adding friction. You're making the automatic behavior harder. You're creating space between the impulse and the action.

Try it for a week. Don't aim for perfection. You'll slip up. You'll make impulse purchases anyway. That's fine. The goal isn't to never spend impulsively again—that's not realistic, and it's probably not even desirable. Sometimes an impulse purchase is fine. Sometimes you see something you want and you buy it and it makes you happy and that's okay.

The goal is to spend impulsively less often. To create enough space between the urge and the action that you can make a conscious choice instead of just reacting.

After a week, assess. Did it work? Even a little?

If yes, keep going. Maybe add another layer. If you started with just deleting payment info, add the waiting period. If you started with the waiting period, add the annoying task. Build the system gradually so it doesn't feel overwhelming.

If no, adjust. This isn't a one-size-fits-all system. It's a framework you customize based on your own patterns.

Pay attention to when you're most vulnerable. Is it late at night? When you're scrolling social media? After a stressful day at work? Right after payday when you feel flush?

Once you know when the impulses hit hardest, you can build friction specifically around those moments.

For me, it's Sunday evenings. I don't know why. Something about the weekend ending and Monday looming makes me want to buy things. It's like I'm trying to extend the weekend by giving myself little gifts, even though that doesn't actually work. So Sunday evenings are when I'm strictest with myself. I don't browse shopping sites. I don't check email where promotional messages might be waiting. I do something else—read, go for a walk, call a friend. I avoid the situations that trigger the impulse in the first place.

That's actually a fourth layer I didn't mention earlier: remove the trigger, not just the ease of purchase. Sometimes the best friction is avoiding the temptation entirely.

If Instagram shopping is your weakness, delete Instagram. Or at least delete it from your phone and only access it from a computer. If late-night scrolling is when you're most vulnerable, put your phone in another room before bed. If sales emails get you, unsubscribe from all of them. Not just the ones from stores you're trying to avoid—all of them. If a sale is good enough, you'll hear about it some other way.

I'm not saying you need to live like a monk. You don't need to delete every app and avoid every store and never look at the internet again. But you do need to be honest about what triggers you. And then you need to make those triggers harder to access.

There's a broader point here that's easy to miss if you're focused on the tactical details of waiting periods and deleted payment info.

Friction isn't really about spending. It's about attention.

Every time you make an impulsive purchase, you're letting some algorithm decide what you pay attention to. You're letting a company's profit motive dictate what feels urgent to you. You see an ad, or a product placement, or a recommendation based on your browsing history, and suddenly you're thinking about something you weren't thinking about five minutes ago. Suddenly you want something you didn't want before.

That's not random. That's not you discovering something you needed. That's engineered desire.

The companies that are best at this—Amazon, Instagram, TikTok—have figured out how to make their recommendations feel like your own idea. The algorithm is so good at predicting what you'll like that when you see it, it doesn't feel like an ad. It feels like serendipity. *Oh, I've been wanting something like that.* No, you haven't. You wanted it starting approximately three seconds ago when you saw it.

Adding friction breaks that spell. It creates distance between the engineered desire and your actual wants. It gives you time to ask: did I want this before I saw it, or do I want it because someone showed it to me?

Most of the time, it's the latter.

And once you see that pattern, once you really internalize how much of your desire is manufactured, it changes how you relate to shopping entirely. You start to see the machinery. You start to notice when you're being manipulated. And manipulation is a lot less effective when you can see it happening.

Sarah told me something interesting after she'd been using her friction system for about three months. She said Instagram was less fun now. Not because she'd deleted it or limited her time on it—she was still scrolling, still seeing the same kinds of posts. But the products didn't pull her in the same way anymore. She'd see something and think, *Oh, they want me to want that.* And once you're thinking that way, the magic is gone.

She didn't mean this as a complaint. She meant it as a revelation. The products hadn't changed. Her attention had. She wasn't being manipulated anymore, or at least not as easily, and it turned out that most of what she thought she wanted was just manufactured desire dressed up as personal preference.

The friction gave her that distance. The waiting period, the deleted payment info, the annoying tasks—they weren't just stopping her from buying things she didn't need. They were training her to see the difference between what she actually wanted and what she'd been sold.

That's the real force multiplier. Not just saving money, though that happens. Not just feeling more in control, though that happens too. It's reclaiming your attention from systems designed to capture it. It's learning to want things on your own terms instead of on theirs.

One more thing before we move on.

You might be wondering if this is sustainable. If adding all this friction is going to make your life so inconvenient that you eventually give up and go back to the frictionless path.

Honest answer? It might. Some people try this for a week and decide it's not worth it. They'd rather have the ease of one-click purchasing than the control that friction gives them. And that's fine. You get to decide what matters to you.

But most people, once they've felt the difference, don't want to go back.

Because here's what happens: at first, the friction feels annoying. You have to type in your credit card number and it feels like a hassle. You have to wait 48 hours and it feels like you're denying yourself something you want. You have to text a friend or go for a walk or calculate your hourly rate and it feels like unnecessary work.

But after a few weeks, the friction stops feeling like a barrier and starts feeling like a buffer. Like protection. You're not fighting against it—it's working for you. It's keeping you from doing something you'll regret. It's giving you time to make better choices.

And then something shifts. The old way—the one-click, instant-purchase, no-friction way—starts to feel dangerous. You see other people buying things impulsively and you think, *I used to do that. I used to let that happen to me.* And you're glad you don't anymore.

That's when the system becomes sustainable. When it stops being something you're forcing yourself to do and starts being something you want to protect. When the friction isn't the hard part anymore—going back to frictionless would be the hard part.

Sarah's at that point now. She still has a want list. She still makes herself wait. She still calculates how many hours of teaching something costs. But she doesn't think about it as a system she's following anymore. It's just how she buys things now. The old way—see it, want it, buy it—feels reckless to her. She tried buying something without the waiting period a few months ago, just to see if she still could, and she felt anxious the whole time. Like she'd skipped a step, forgotten to check something important.

The friction had become the default. The old frictionless path was now the effortful choice.

That's what I want for you. Not a system you white-knuckle your way through for a month before giving up. A new default. A new normal. A way of spending that feels deliberate instead of automatic, controlled instead of reactive, yours instead of theirs.

And once you have that—once you've reclaimed that space between wanting and having—you'll wonder how you ever lived without it.

I never did delete my Amazon account. I made it to confirmation screen six and stopped. But sitting there, watching that seventh screen load, I realized something: I couldn't just remove the problem. I had to build something that survived it.

Chapter 4: The Fun Money Account System

You know that feeling when you've been so good? Days, maybe weeks of saying no to yourself. Scrolling past the thing. Closing the tab. Walking out of the store empty-handed while your brain screams that you deserve this, you earned it. And then one Tuesday night, something breaks.

And then one night—Tuesday, probably, because the catastrophes always happen on Tuesdays—something breaks.

My sister didn't plan to buy the handbag. She'd been resisting it for months, had made it into this whole symbol of her newfound financial discipline. Proof she was changing. But then she had a bad day at work, poured a second glass of wine, and at 11:47 PM her phone lit up with a notification about a sale ending at midnight. Eight hundred dollars. Final sale, no returns.

She called me crying.

Not because eight hundred dollars would ruin her financially—she could technically afford it. But because this was her third attempt at quitting impulse buying cold turkey, and each time the pattern was identical: intense restriction, mounting pressure, spectacular collapse. The first attempt lasted eleven days before she bought three hundred dollars worth of clothes she never wore. Second attempt, sixteen days before a home décor spree. This time she'd made it almost three weeks. Almost.

The next day she showed up at my apartment with the bag still in its dust cover, tags attached, and set it on my kitchen counter like evidence.

"I can't even return it," she said.

We sat there looking at this beautiful, expensive object she'd wanted for months and now felt sick about owning. And that's when I stopped thinking about her willpower and started thinking about the system itself.

Because here's what nobody tells you about budgeting, what all those financial advice columns and debt-free influencers seem to miss: restriction alone has never worked. Will never work. You can build all the friction you want—delete apps, block websites, freeze your credit card in actual ice like you're living in some kind of personal finance performance art piece—but if you don't give yourself permission to spend *somewhere*, you're not building a budget.

You're building a bomb.

Think about every diet you've ever tried. The ones where you cut out entire food groups, where you told yourself you'd never eat bread again, never touch sugar, never enjoy anything that tastes good. How did those go?

Right.

Maybe you lasted a week. Maybe two. Maybe if you were exceptionally committed and possibly also exceptionally miserable, you made it a month. But eventually you didn't just eat bread—you ate half a loaf standing at the kitchen counter at 9 PM, barely tasting it, just shoveling it in because the dam broke and you might as well, you already failed, might as well make it count.

Money works the same way. Right now you're probably trying to hold back a flood with sandbags. Telling yourself not that, not now, maybe later, probably never. White-knuckling your way through Target. And maybe you win that fight for a while. But eventually—because you're human, not a budgeting robot—the dam breaks. And when it does, you don't just buy the thing you've been resisting. You buy that *and* three other things you weren't even thinking about. The floodgates are open. You've already failed. Might as well get free shipping.

I've watched this pattern play out so many times I've lost count. With my sister. With friends. With myself, if we're being honest here.

There was a year I decided I wasn't going to spend money on anything "unnecessary" until I'd saved three months of expenses. Noble goal, right? Responsible. Adult.

I lasted six weeks before I walked into a bookstore just to browse—just to *browse*, I told myself, like I was someone who could walk into a bookstore and not buy anything—and walked out with one hundred and forty dollars worth of books. Then, because I'd already broken my rule, I stopped for the expensive coffee. And then I saw this lamp in a shop window that would be perfect for my reading corner. By the end of the day I'd spent over two hundred dollars and felt worse than if I'd just been buying books all along.

Because it wasn't just about the money. It was about the failure. The proof that I couldn't stick to anything.

But the problem wasn't my willpower. It was the system. I'd set myself up to fail by trying to eliminate all pleasure spending, which is about as realistic as trying to eliminate all carbohydrates or never looking at your phone again. It might work for a hot minute. It's not sustainable.

And that's where the Fun Money Account comes in. Not as another restriction. As the opposite. As structured permission. As an outlet valve on the pressure cooker before it explodes.

The concept is straightforward: you allocate a specific amount of money each month for spontaneous, guilt-free spending. A truly fixed amount. And once it's allocated, it's yours to use however you want. No justification required. No mental gymnastics about whether you "deserve" it.

Want the ridiculous novelty mug shaped like a T-Rex? Go for it. See a concert ticket for a band you haven't thought about since college? Absolutely. Spot a vintage leather jacket at the thrift store that you definitely don't need but would look amazing on you? If it fits within your Fun Money allocation, you don't need to think about it. You just buy it.

If it doesn't fit, either it waits until next month or you decide whether it's worth cutting something else.

I know what you're thinking. I can hear it from here.

Isn't this just enabling the problem? Giving myself permission to impulse buy?

Here's the thing, though. The impulse buying is already happening. Right now, without this system, you're impulse buying *and* feeling terrible about it. You're spending money you haven't allocated, then lying awake at 2 AM doing mental math on whether you can still pay the electric bill. You're adding things to your cart at midnight and hitting purchase and then immediately feeling that stomach-drop of regret.

The Fun Money Account doesn't create impulse spending. It contains it.

It separates the "want" spending from the "need" spending and prevents those little treats from snowballing into the kind of financial chaos that keeps you up at night refreshing your bank account balance.

Because here's what really happens when you try to restrict all fun: you tell yourself you'll reward yourself "later." Once you've paid off the student loans. Once you've saved ten thousand dollars. Once you get the promotion. Once you hit some milestone that keeps receding like the horizon line.

Meanwhile you're miserable. You're watching everyone else seem to enjoy their lives while you eat rice and beans for the fourth night in a row and try to convince yourself that this is character-building. And eventually—because again, human, not robot—you snap.

You don't just buy one thing. You buy everything. You go on a spree. And then you feel so guilty about it that you swing back to restriction, and the whole cycle starts over.

Delayed gratification sounds great in a TED talk. But human beings also need a little bit of immediate pleasure. We're wired for it. The dopamine hit from a small purchase isn't a character flaw—it's neurobiology. Your brain lights up when you see something new and interesting. That response kept our ancestors motivated to explore, to find new food sources, to build better tools, to generally stay alive. It's not a bug. It's a feature.

The modern problem is that this ancient wiring now fires when you're scrolling Instagram at midnight and an ad knows exactly what you've been looking at for the past week and offers you free shipping if you buy in the next hour.

Deprivation doesn't lead to discipline. It leads to overspending down the line. It creates this binge-and-restrict cycle that leaves you feeling worse off than before—plus guilty, plus convinced you're "bad with money."

You're not bad with money. You're just using a system that fights against how your brain actually works instead of working with it.

So let's talk numbers. How much should you actually allocate?

There's no magic formula here, no perfect percentage that works for everyone. It varies wildly depending on your income, your fixed expenses, your debt situation, where you live, what brings you joy, whether you have kids, whether you're supporting other people, a thousand different factors.

But a good starting point is five to ten percent of your after-tax monthly income.

And here's something that might surprise you: if you're really struggling with impulse spending right now, if you're in the middle of that binge-restrict cycle, you might want to lean toward the higher end initially.

I know. It sounds backward. Shouldn't you be *restricting* more if you have a problem?

But remember—restriction is what's been failing you. What you need isn't more deprivation. It's containment. A bigger Fun Money allocation at the start can prevent the pressure-cooker effect while you're building the habit of working within boundaries. You're creating a wide enough channel that the pressure can release without destroying everything downstream.

You can always adjust down later once the system is working. But if you start too restrictive, you'll trigger the same binge-restrict pattern you're trying to escape.

On the other hand, if you're generally pretty disciplined and you're just trying to add more structure, you can start lower and adjust as needed. The goal isn't deprivation. It's sustainability.

Let me show you what this looked like for Sarah.

Sarah is thirty-two, teaches high school English, and was consistently overspending on online shopping when she was stressed. And teaching high school English meant she was stressed a lot. After a day of managing one hundred and fifty teenagers with varying degrees of interest in *The Great Gatsby* and even less interest in using the semicolon correctly, she'd come home, pour a glass of wine, open her laptop, and just... browse.

She'd justify it with phrases that probably sound familiar. "I deserve this." "It's just a little treat." "I work hard."

A forty-dollar candle that smelled like "Woodland Berry" and came in a ceramic vessel she'd definitely reuse for something. A sweater in a color she already owned three versions of. Organizational bins for a closet reorganization project she'd been planning for eight months and would probably never actually start. A subscription box that promised to "curate her best life" and mostly delivered samples of face cream.

After tracking her spending for a month—the exercise from Chapter 1, the one where you actually look at every single transaction instead of just vibing your way through your bank statement—she realized she was averaging around three hundred dollars a month on this stuff. Clothes she never wore. Gadgets that gathered dust. Things that seemed essential at 11 PM on a Wednesday and baffling by Friday morning.

It wasn't necessarily the *amount* that was the problem. Three hundred dollars out of her forty-five-hundred-dollar monthly take-home wasn't going to bankrupt her. It was the lack of control. The feeling of being hijacked by her own brain. The guilt that gnawed at her every time she opened her credit card statement and saw the damage itemized.

But here's what that lack of control was actually costing her. The real number. The one she'd been avoiding looking at.

Sarah was carrying a forty-two-hundred-dollar balance on her credit card at 19.99% APR. She'd accumulated it over about eighteen months—thirty dollars here, eighty there, until it had grown into this thing she couldn't quite look at directly. Every month she made the minimum payment of around a hundred dollars, which meant she was mostly just paying interest. The principal barely budged.

At that rate, paying minimums, it would take her over seven years to pay off the balance.

Seven years.

And over that time, she'd end up paying nearly three thousand dollars in interest alone.

Think about that for a second. Three thousand dollars. That's a vacation to Europe. A used car. A year's worth of the "treats" she was supposedly enjoying. Except she wasn't enjoying them. She was feeling guilty about them. And they were costing her thousands of dollars in interest on top of the original price.

And every month, she kept adding another three hundred dollars in impulse purchases to that balance. So the number never went down. She was on a treadmill, running hard, staying exactly in place.

This is what restriction-without-structure actually costs. Not just money. Time. Years of your life paying interest on a candle you bought when you were stressed about work.

Sarah's take-home pay is forty-five hundred dollars a month. Using the ten percent guideline, her initial Fun Money allocation would be four hundred and fifty dollars.

She opened a separate online savings account—one of those high-yield accounts from an online bank, took maybe ten minutes to set up—and labeled it "Fun Money" in her banking app. Some banks let you nickname accounts, which is weirdly satisfying. She could have called it "Chaos Fund" or "Bad Decisions Money" or "The Woodland Berry Candle Memorial Fund." She went with the straightforward option.

Each month, on payday, she set up an automatic transfer of four fifty into that account.

Now here's where it gets important, the part you can't skip: this money isn't for emergencies. It's not for bills or groceries or gas or anything sensible. It's *only* for fun stuff. The candles. The concert tickets. The face cream from TikTok. The organizational bins she'll probably never use.

And once it's gone, it's gone until next month.

That limitation is crucial. It's not a suggestion. It's the entire point. It forces you to prioritize your wants and make conscious choices about how you spend your play money. It turns impulse buying into intentional buying. You're still buying the thing. You're just choosing it instead of being ambushed by it.

The first few weeks were challenging. Sarah felt the urge to buy things outside her Fun Money account. A pair of shoes she'd been eyeing. A last-minute weekend trip her friends were planning. Her brain kept trying to run the old program: see thing, want thing, buy thing, feel bad.

But she'd built a system that made the choice clearer.

She could see her Fun Money balance. She could see that she had four hundred and fifty dollars allocated for whatever struck her fancy. And she could also see that those shoes would cost a hundred and twenty dollars, which would leave her with three hundred and thirty for the rest of the month.

Was it worth it?

Sometimes yes. Sometimes no. But now she was *choosing*, not just reacting. Not just hitting "buy now" at midnight and hoping for the best.

She started using her Fun Money for things she genuinely enjoyed. A monthly massage—the kind where they use hot stones and she walks out feeling like a new person. Tickets to a local theater performance. A new book and a cozy blanket for reading on Sunday afternoons. She even used some of it to take an online pottery class, something she'd always wanted to try but had convinced herself was "frivolous."

(Turns out spending money on things you've always wanted to try isn't frivolous. It's living your life. But that's a different conversation.)

The key was that she wasn't feeling guilty about spending the money because it had already been budgeted for. It was *supposed* to be spent. That mental shift—from "I shouldn't be doing this" to "This is exactly what this money is for"—changed everything.

The system isn't foolproof. Sarah occasionally blew through her Fun Money faster than expected. There was a particularly rough week in February—budget cuts at school, a fight with her sister, her car making a weird noise that turned out to be nothing but stressed her out for three days anyway—where she stress-bought three different candles and a weighted blanket. By the third week of the month she had forty-seven dollars left in Fun Money.

But here's what didn't happen: she didn't spiral. She didn't say "well I've already blown it so I might as well keep going." She didn't add four more things to her cart to hit the free shipping threshold. She simply acknowledged it and made a conscious effort to be more mindful with her remaining funds.

She found herself thinking twice before making purchases. Not because she was depriving herself. Because she wanted to get the most enjoyment out of her limited Fun Money budget.

And here's what happened to that credit card balance:

Within three months of implementing the Fun Money Account, Sarah redirected a hundred and fifty dollars a month from those old impulse purchases—the ones that used to just vanish into the void of random online shopping—toward her credit card debt. That's a hundred fifty on top of her minimum payment, going straight to principal.

Instead of seven years, she was now on track to pay off the balance in under three years.

Instead of paying three thousand dollars in interest, she'd pay closer to eight hundred.

She saved herself twenty-two hundred dollars and four years of stress. Not by becoming a different person. Not by developing superhuman willpower. Just by designing a different system. One that worked with her brain instead of against it.

Let me walk you through how to set this up for yourself. Four steps. We're going to do this like we're sitting across from each other with coffee and you're actually going to implement this, not just read about it and think "yeah I should do that" and then never do it.

Step One: Calculate Your Allocation

Start with five to ten percent of your after-tax monthly income. Be realistic about what you can comfortably afford. If you're unsure, start lower and adjust upward as needed.

But before you just pick a number out of thin air, do this: grab your bank statements from the last two months.

I know you don't want to. Look anyway.

Figure out what you're *actually* spending on impulse buys right now. Not what you think you should be spending. Not what you wish you were spending. What you are actually, currently, in reality spending.

That's your baseline. The truth.

Go line by line if you have to. The eight dollars here for a smoothie you didn't plan on. The thirty-five dollars there for the face cream you saw on TikTok. The sixty-seven dollars for the thing you bought at Target when you only went in for toothpaste.

(Why is it always toothpaste? Why do we never just buy the toothpaste and leave? Is there a conspiracy? Are they pumping something through the vents?)

Add it all up. Be honest with yourself. Round up if you're not sure.

If it's four hundred dollars and you make four thousand a month, that's ten percent. If it feels too high—and it might, seeing it all added up in one number can be sobering—you can start at three hundred or even two fifty. The point is to start somewhere honest, not somewhere aspirational. Not where you think you "should" be, but where you actually are.

Step Two: Open a Dedicated Account

This is essential. Non-negotiable. People always think they can skip this step. They can't.

Don't just earmark a portion of your checking account. Don't just tell yourself "okay, three hundred of the money in my checking account is for fun stuff." That doesn't work. Your brain doesn't work that way. Money in your checking account is just money. It all looks the same. It all spends the same.

Open a separate savings account or online account specifically for Fun Money.

The physical separation reinforces the mental separation between "needs" and "wants." Most banks let you do this online in about ten minutes. Some even let you nickname the account. My friend Rachel calls hers "Chaos Fund." My friend Marcus calls his "Bad Decisions Money." My sister eventually named hers "The Handbag Fund" as a reminder of what happens when you don't have a system.

I use a high-yield savings account from one of those online banks—Ally, Marcus by Goldman Sachs, Capital One 360, there are several options. You get a tiny bit of interest, not much but better than nothing. And the fact that transfers take a day or two actually helps. It adds just enough friction that you won't drain the account on a whim at 11 PM, but not so much that you can't access it when you genuinely want to make a purchase.

Step Three: Automate the Transfer

Set up an automatic transfer from your main account to your Fun Money account on payday. Not the day after. Not when you remember. The same day your paycheck deposits.

This ensures the money is allocated before you have a chance to spend it elsewhere. Before you even see it sitting there in your checking account looking spendable.

Automation is your friend here. You're not relying on remembering to do it each month. You're not relying on having the discipline to manually move money around when you're tired or stressed or distracted. You're building a system that runs whether you're paying attention or not.

Most banks let you set this up in the same interface where you opened the account. Recurring transfer. Same day every month (or every two weeks, depending on your pay schedule). Set it and forget it.

This is the difference between a system and a goal. Goals require constant willpower and attention. Systems just run.

Step Four: Establish Clear Rules

Define what constitutes "fun" spending for you specifically. Is dining out included, or does that come from a different budget category? What about hobbies? Entertainment subscriptions? Coffee shops? Books? The concert tickets? The vintage leather jacket?

The more specific you are, the easier it will be to stick to the system. You won't have to renegotiate with yourself every single time you want to buy something.

Sarah decided that her Fun Money covered: online shopping for non-essentials, dining out beyond her regular grocery budget (she allocated two hundred a month for groceries and basic meal planning; anything on top of that came from Fun Money), hobby supplies, entertainment like movies or concerts or books, and "random stuff I just want."

Her regular budget covered: groceries, her one Netflix subscription that she shared with her sister, and her weekday morning coffee shop runs. She gave herself forty dollars a month for the coffee because it was a daily routine that brought her genuine joy and she didn't want to have to think about it or track it. It was just part of her life.

Your rules will be different. That's fine. That's the entire point. This isn't a one-size-fits-all template. It's a framework you customize.

Just write your rules down somewhere. Notes app. Sticky note on your bathroom mirror. Document on your laptop. Wherever you'll actually see it when you need it. So you're not re-deciding every time.

The Fun Money Account isn't just about preventing overspending. It's about building a healthier relationship with money. It allows you to enjoy life without sacrificing your financial goals. When you give yourself permission to spend on things that bring you joy—within reasonable, predetermined limits—you eliminate the guilt and shame that usually come with impulse purchases.

And that elimination of guilt, that permission structure, makes it exponentially easier to stay on track with your overall budget and work toward long-term financial security.

It's about finding the balance between discipline and indulgence. Between being responsible and being human. Between having goals and having a life worth living while you work toward those goals.

Let me show you one more example, because I want you to see how this works across different income levels and spending patterns.

David earns six thousand dollars a month after taxes. He's a software developer, lives alone in a one-bedroom apartment, works from home most days, and has a very specific weakness: gadgets.

Electronics. Smart home devices. The latest noise-canceling headphones even though the ones he bought six months ago work perfectly fine. A mechanical keyboard with customizable RGB lighting because the reviews said it would "transform his workspace." A standing desk converter he used for three weeks before it became a shelf for books and empty coffee mugs. A smart speaker that promised to integrate with everything and mostly just tells him the weather when he didn't ask.

After reviewing his spending—something he'd been avoiding for about two years because looking at it felt too much like admitting he had a problem—he realized he was spending about six hundred dollars a month on impulsive tech purchases.

Some of it he used. A lot of it sat in boxes in his closet, still sealed. There was a three-hundred-dollar smart speaker system still in the packaging from four months ago. A fitness tracker he'd bought during a moment of ambitious New Year optimism, worn twice.

Six hundred dollars a month. Seventy-two hundred dollars a year. On stuff he mostly didn't use.

When he actually calculated it out, when he saw that number—seventy-two hundred dollars—something shifted. That was a down payment on a car. A really nice vacation. A substantial chunk toward the emergency fund he kept telling himself he'd build "eventually."

David set his Fun Money allocation at four hundred dollars a month, about 6.7% of his income. Lower than the ten percent guideline because he wanted to redirect some of that spending toward savings, but high enough that he didn't feel deprived.

The first month was hard. He saw a new tablet release and had to talk himself out of buying it. He closed approximately seventeen browser tabs of product reviews for things he suddenly "needed." His Amazon cart had twenty-three items in it at one point.

But the Fun Money Account forced him to prioritize. Did he want the tablet more than he wanted the new headphones? More than the smart light system he'd been eyeing? More than keeping some buffer for whatever new thing would inevitably catch his attention later in the month?

He started asking himself a new question before every purchase: "Will I actually use this, or do I just like the idea of owning it?"

Turns out, the answer was "just like the idea of owning it" about seventy percent of the time.

By month three, David had redirected two hundred dollars a month from gadget purchases into a high-yield savings account. By month six, he had twelve hundred dollars saved—emergency fund money, the kind that sits there boring and unused until the day you desperately need it and it saves you from catastrophe.

He still bought gadgets. He used his Fun Money on a really nice pair of headphones he uses every single day. A mechanical keyboard he genuinely loves. A smart home hub that he actually set up and integrated. The difference was that now he was choosing. He was asking himself what he really wanted, what would actually improve his life, instead of just buying everything that looked cool in a YouTube review.

The Fun Money Account gave him something he didn't expect: clarity. Permission to spend, yes, but also permission to *not* spend without feeling like he was depriving himself.

Here's what I want you to understand: the Fun Money Account is permission and boundaries at the same time. It's structured freedom. It's the difference between "I can't buy anything" (which doesn't work) and "I can buy anything I want as long as it fits within this predetermined amount" (which does).

You're not eliminating impulse spending. You're not turning yourself into some kind of ascetic monk who owns three shirts and eats lentils for every meal. You're redirecting the impulse through a channel that you control.

Some months you'll use all of it. Some months you won't. Some months you'll blow through it in two weeks and spend the rest of the month window-shopping without buying. Some months you'll be surprised to find money left over.

The pattern will vary. That's normal. That's human.

What won't vary—if you stick with the system—is the guilt. That goes away. Replaced by something better: choice.

You chose to allocate this money. You chose what to spend it on. You chose to wait when something didn't fit. You chose to redirect money toward your credit card or your savings or your rent or whatever else matters to you.

You're not being controlled by algorithms designed to extract money from you at your weakest moments. You're not being hijacked by targeted ads at midnight. You're not spiraling through the binge-restrict cycle wondering why you can't just be normal about money.

You're running a system. And the system is working for you, not against you.

Set it up this week. Not "soon." Not "when things calm down." This week. Open the account. Calculate the number. Automate the transfer. Write down your rules.

And then next month, when you want something—really want it, that deep want that feels like need—you'll have a different question to ask yourself. Not "should I?" but "does this fit?" Not "am I allowed?" but "is this what I want to use my permission for?"

That question, that shift, changes everything.

My sister kept the handbag. Still uses it. That's not the problem. The problem was that buying it felt like failure, and feeling like a failure made her give up on the budget entirely.

My sister used her first Fun Money account to buy a scarf. Not the handbag. A scarf. Thirty-eight dollars. She still has it. But the scarf didn't solve the problem of the phone in her hand at 11 PM, Instagram open, scrolling.

Chapter 5: Cue Management & Digital Detox

What if I told you the problem isn't that you lack willpower—it's that your phone knows exactly when you're tired, bored, or stressed, and that's when it decides to show you the thing you've been resisting all week?

Email notification. "Your order has shipped."

This was maybe my fourth or fifth budgeting workshop. I was still nervous before every session, still half-convinced someone would raise their hand and ask a question that would expose me as someone who didn't actually have all the answers. Still reading from slides I'd rewritten three times because I couldn't tell if they were helpful or just me trying to sound like I knew what I was talking about.

I glanced at my phone reflexively. The way you do even when you're supposed to be focused on something else, even when you're literally in the middle of teaching other people how to be better with money.

Meal-planning app. My third that month.

I hadn't opened either of the previous two past day two.

The workshop participants didn't notice—I kept talking, advanced to the next slide, made a joke about grocery store impulse buys that got a decent laugh—but I knew. And the thing that struck me wasn't the hypocrisy, exactly, though that was definitely part of it. What got me was how completely *absent* I'd been from the decision. I had seen an ad, probably while scrolling Instagram during a break between client calls, clicked through, entered my payment information, confirmed, and completely forgotten about it by the time the shipping notification arrived.

There was no decision point. No moment where I thought "Do I need this?" No part of my brain that said "Hey, remember how you already bought two of these and didn't use either one?"

Just: stimulus -> response -> done.

That's when something clicked for me about impulse spending. Not while I was researching it, not while I was writing workshop materials, but while I was actively doing the thing I was teaching people not to do. The problem isn't willpower. It's not that you're weak or undisciplined or bad with money.

The problem is you're trying to make conscious choices in a system that's designed to bypass consciousness entirely.

Your brain has learned a shortcut. Stimulus arrives, behavior executes, reward delivers. The loop runs automatically, the same way you don't think about pressing the brake when a traffic light turns red. You just do it. You've done it ten thousand times. It's encoded.

And the frustrating thing—the thing that makes budgeting advice so useless most of the time—is that you can't override an automatic behavior with willpower. Not for long, anyway. Willpower is a limited resource that depletes over the course of the day. Automatic behaviors cost nothing. They're always available. They run in the background while your conscious mind is busy with something else.

So the willpower-based approach to impulse spending—just resist the temptation, just say no, just be stronger—is like telling someone to hold their breath longer when the real problem is they're standing in a room with no oxygen.

You don't need more discipline.

You need to change the room.

But before we talk about changing the room, I want to sit with something for a minute. Because I think most people know intellectually that impulse spending is a problem, but they haven't actually let themselves feel the full weight of what it costs.

You buy something small. It feels inconsequential. You move on.

The purchase disappears into the background of your life. But those purchases aren't isolated events. They're creating a pattern, and that pattern is quietly reshaping your reality in ways you probably haven't stopped to notice.

Think about Sarah for a second—the graphic designer we met earlier who was spending about $300 a month on late-night clothing orders triggered by work stress. That's $3,600 a year. Which doesn't sound life-changing at first, maybe. Like, sure, it's real money, but it's not "buy a house" money or "retire early" money or whatever.

Except here's what that $3,600 actually cost her.

It was the reason she didn't have an emergency fund. Which was the reason she couldn't afford to take two weeks off between jobs when she got laid off from the agency that was burning her out. Which meant she had to take the first offer she got instead of waiting for something better. Which locked her into another job that paid less and stressed her out more, which triggered more impulse spending, which kept the whole cycle running.

It was also the reason she stayed in a relationship six months longer than she should have.

She wanted to leave—had wanted to leave for a while, actually—but she couldn't afford the security deposit and first month's rent on her own place. Because the money that should've been building an exit fund had evaporated into a closet full of clothes she'd bought while feeling trapped.

The impulse spending wasn't just draining her bank account. It was actively trapping her in situations she desperately wanted to leave.

Or look at David—the guy buying tech gadgets he didn't need—from a different angle. It wasn't just wasted money. Every time he bought another pair of wireless earbuds or a mechanical keyboard or some smart home device he'd use exactly once before it became decoration, he was postponing actual meaningful purchases. He wanted to take a ceramics class. He wanted to visit his sister in Portland—they'd been talking about it for two years, kept saying "soon," and it never happened. He wanted to upgrade his design software to the professional tier so he could take on better clients and maybe, eventually, stop working for someone else.

But every time he had money available for those things, it had already evaporated.

Into a drawer full of cables he'd never use. Into gadgets that were supposed to make his life better but mostly just cluttered up his desk.

He wasn't choosing gadgets over ceramics or Portland or better software. He was making a series of small, forgettable purchases that felt like nothing in the moment, and the cumulative effect was that the things he actually cared about never happened.

The emotional cost is harder to quantify but just as real.

There's this specific kind of guilt that comes from impulse spending. Not the dramatic guilt of a major financial mistake—not "oh god I bought a car I can't afford" guilt—but this low-grade shame that hums in the background of your life. Every time you open your credit card statement. Every time someone asks what you did with your paycheck and you genuinely can't account for where it went. Every time you have to decline an invitation because you're "trying to save money" while simultaneously knowing you dropped sixty bucks last week on books you haven't read and a kitchen gadget you used exactly once before it migrated to the back of the cabinet where all the other gadgets live.

You start avoiding looking at your finances altogether.

Because the evidence of your lack of control is just sitting there, undeniable, in rows of transactions you barely remember making. So you don't look. Which means you don't know how bad it is. Which means it gets worse. Which makes you want to look even less.

And maybe the worst part—the part that actually keeps people stuck longer than the money itself—is you lose trust in yourself.

You make plans. This month will be different. I'm going to stick to my budget this time. I'm serious.

And then you break them. Over and over.

Not because you're weak or broken, but because you're trying to solve a design problem with a willpower solution, and willpower runs out around 3 PM on a Tuesday when you're tired and your boss just added another task to your plate and you need something, *anything*, to feel better for five minutes.

But you don't know that's the issue. You just assume you're the issue.

You internalize the failure. You stop believing you're capable of change. You stop making plans at all because what's the point? You'll just break those too.

That's what's actually at stake here. Not just money, though it's definitely money. Your sense of agency. Your ability to build the life you want instead of defaulting to the life your impulses create for you.

So let's talk about cues.

Because once you understand how they work, the whole thing starts to feel less like a character flaw and more like a solvable design problem.

A cue is just your brain being efficient. It creates associations between situations and behaviors so you don't have to consciously think through every single action. Red light means press brake. Alarm goes off means hit snooze. Inbox hits zero means feel accomplished for about three seconds before anxiety kicks in again. Your brain loves shortcuts. It's genuinely trying to help.

Problem is, your brain can't tell the difference between a useful shortcut and a destructive one. Both get encoded the same way. Both feel automatic. Both are really, really hard to override with willpower alone.

Brené Brown wrote about this once—back before she became *the* Brené Brown, before the TED talk hit tens of millions of views, before the Netflix special. She mentioned looking at her credit card statement and seeing seventeen separate purchases from Target in a single month. Not seventeen trips to the store. Seventeen individual online orders. Each one its own transaction. Each one its own shipping notification. Each one its own moment of clicking "confirm purchase" and moving on with her day.

Small stuff, mostly. Throw pillows. Decorative baskets. Three different kinds of storage containers for her office supplies. The kind of purchases that feel reasonable in the moment—it's just $19.99, and besides, you need it, right?—but stack up to real money when you're placing them twice a week.

What bothered her wasn't the spending itself. It was the autopilot nature of it. She'd be working on a research paper, hit a frustrating section where the data wasn't cooperating, and suddenly find herself browsing Target's home goods section. Twenty minutes later she'd snap out of it with a confirmation email in her inbox and zero memory of actually deciding to shop.

Her brain had learned a shortcut: frustration + screen = browse + buy = temporary relief.

She wasn't making choices. She was running a program.

And that's the thing people miss about impulse spending. It's not a series of bad choices. It's an automated response to specific triggers that you're not even consciously registering most of the time. The decision happens before you realize there's a decision to make.

Which means willpower-based solutions are fighting the wrong battle. You can't white-knuckle your way through every moment of temptation when most of the time you don't even register that you're being tempted.

You need to go upstream. You need to disrupt the cue before it triggers the behavior.

Start by identifying your specific cues. And they *are* specific—way more specific than you probably think.

Most people know social media is a trigger, but “social media” is too broad to be useful. Instagram ads for home décor hit different than TikTok videos about productivity tools, which hit different than Facebook marketplace browsing when you’re supposedly looking for a used bookshelf but somehow end up considering a vintage typewriter you absolutely do not need and have nowhere to put.

The pattern isn’t just *platform*. It’s platform + emotional state + time of day + what else is happening in your life + whether you ate lunch + how that conversation with your coworker went + a dozen other variables your conscious mind isn’t tracking but your brain absolutely is.

Here’s what I want you to do for one week: track your urges.

Not your spending. Your *urges*.

Every time you feel the pull to buy something—before you actually purchase, before you even add it to cart, the moment you feel that little tug toward shopping—write down:

- Where you are, physically and digitally. At your desk? On the couch? In bed? On Instagram? Amazon? Some clothing brand’s website you don’t remember navigating to? - What time it is. Down to the minute if you can. - What you were doing right before the urge hit. Working? Watching TV? Scrolling? Talking to someone? Sitting in traffic? - How you're feeling. Tired, anxious, bored, frustrated, excited, vindicated, petty, whatever. Don't edit. Don't make it sound better than it is. Just name it. - Whether you're alone or with people. - What you're avoiding by shopping right now. And there's always something. Always. Even if it's just "I'm avoiding going to bed because then tomorrow will come."

You're not trying to resist the urges during this week. You're just observing them. Treating yourself like a subject in a study. Curiosity, not criticism. No judgment, just data collection.

Write it down every single time. Even if it's the fifth urge that day. Even if you're sick of writing it down. Especially if you're sick of writing it down, actually, because that repetition is data too.

After a week, patterns emerge.

Maybe you're vulnerable every day around 3 PM when your energy crashes and you start browsing as a pick-me-up. Maybe it's Sunday evenings when you're dreading the week ahead and trying to feel like you're doing *something* productive even if it's just buying a new notebook that will definitely make you more organized this time. Maybe it's specifically after phone calls with your mother. Or when you're waiting for feedback on a project and trying to distract yourself from the anxiety. Or when you see someone else's vacation photos and suddenly need a new swimsuit even though you have no trips planned and it's February.

The cues are usually way more specific than "I was on Instagram."

It's "I was on Instagram at 11 PM after a frustrating day when I couldn't sleep and my partner was already asleep and I felt lonely and the house was too quiet and scrolling felt like being around people without having to be around people."

Once you know your specific triggers, you can start designing them out of your environment.

This is where most advice goes wrong. They tell you to delete social media entirely. Never shop online again. Go full minimalist ascetic monk mode. Which is about as realistic as telling someone to never feel stressed.

You're not a monk. You live in the world. The world has Instagram in it. The world has Amazon. You're going to interact with these things.

You're not trying to eliminate the emotional states that trigger shopping. You can't eliminate frustration or boredom or anxiety. Those are part of being human.

You're trying to break the automatic connection between those states and the shopping behavior.

Let's get tactical.

Say Instagram ads are a major trigger for you. Specifically in the evening when you're winding down and your defenses are low and everything looks better in that perfectly curated photo. You don't want to delete Instagram—you actually enjoy keeping up with friends, and besides, deleting it feels like admitting defeat—but you're tired of the constant product pitches.

First: unfollow every single account that exists primarily to sell you things.

Influencers who do constant "swipe up to shop" posts. Brands you followed because you liked one product once and now they're in your feed every day reminding you of other things you don't own. Accounts that curate products and gift guides. Those "aesthetic" accounts that are just disguised advertising. Anyone whose business model depends on making you feel like you're missing out on things you don't have.

It feels harsh. Especially if you genuinely like their content. But ask yourself honestly: does seeing their posts make you feel satisfied with what you own, or does it create this low-grade sense that you're falling behind?

You know the answer.

Then—and this is the part people skip—replace them with accounts that fill the same psychological need without the spending trigger.

If you followed home décor influencers, follow people who post about decorating with what you already own. Or DIY projects using free materials. Or beautiful spaces in museums or historical sites that nobody's trying to sell you. If you followed fashion accounts, switch to vintage fashion history or sewing tutorials or style challenges using existing wardrobes. You still get the visual pleasure, the inspiration, the sense of "oh that's cool." You just removed the purchase funnel.

You're not depriving yourself of the content category you enjoy. You're just removing the part that's designed to make you feel inadequate until you buy something.

For email marketing, the fix is simpler and more drastic: unsubscribe from everything.

All of it.

Every retail newsletter. Every promotional email. Every "you left something in your cart" reminder. Every "just for you" sale. Every "we miss you" discount code. Every "exclusive early access" announcement. Every single one.

It takes an afternoon. Maybe two afternoons if you've been subscribed to retail emails for years. Open your inbox, search for "unsubscribe," and just start clicking. Over and over. It's tedious. Your hand will cramp. You'll get bored. Do it anyway.

The immediate reduction in daily temptation is substantial.

You're not missing out on deals. Here's the truth nobody wants to hear: if you need something specific, you can seek out sales when you're ready to buy. Retail sales happen constantly. Every week is some kind of sale. Black Friday deals. Cyber Monday. End-of-season clearance. New-season preview. Holiday sales. We-haven't-had-a-sale-in-three-days sales. You don't need to be alerted the instant a promotion goes live.

And the vast majority of promotional emails aren't alerting you to deals on things you need anyway. They're creating desire for things you don't, then offering you a discount to manufacture urgency.

"24 hours only!"

Except there's another sale starting the second this one ends. There's always another sale.

The scarcity is fake. The need is fake. The urgency is fake. The only thing that's real is the money leaving your account.

Now let's talk about the platforms themselves. Because they're not neutral ground.

Amazon's interface is designed—designed by very smart people who study consumer psychology for a living—to maximize the chance you'll buy additional things beyond what you came for.

The "frequently bought together" suggestions. The "customers also viewed" carousel. The entire "recommended for you" homepage. The way they show you what's in your cart but also what's in your "save for later" list but also what you browsed yesterday but didn't buy. All of it exists to extend your browsing session and increase your cart size.

You cannot eliminate that design through willpower. You can eliminate your exposure to it.

Delete the Amazon app from your phone.

Fully delete it. Not "move it to a folder on the third screen." Not "turn off notifications." Delete.

If you need to order something, do it from a desktop browser. Which adds just enough friction—go to computer, open browser, navigate to site, log in—to disrupt the autopilot behavior.

The difference is small. But it's often enough to interrupt the impulse loop.

You're not banning yourself from Amazon. You're just making it slightly less frictionless. And friction, as we've talked about, is your friend here.

Because here's what actually happens with most impulse purchases: you're lying in bed, half-asleep, scrolling through something that caught your attention, and suddenly you're three taps away from buying something you'll barely remember ordering when it shows up on your doorstep four days later.

Phone. App. Product. Cart. Checkout. Confirm. Done.

The whole transaction takes maybe ninety seconds. Maybe less if you have one-click ordering enabled (which you should absolutely turn off, by the way—go into your account settings right now and disable it, I'll wait).

One of the things that surprised me when I started tracking my own spending patterns was how many purchases I made in the ten minutes before I actually fell asleep. Not while I was lying in bed reading or watching something. While I was actively *trying* to fall asleep. Like, eyes closed, lying there in the dark, not sleeping yet, picking up my phone "just to check one thing," and then somehow ending up on a product page adding something to cart.

I think I was trying to give my brain something to do other than spiral about whatever I was anxious about that day. Which, fine, I get it, brains are annoying like that. But there are cheaper ways to distract yourself from anxiety than buying a book you'll never read about a topic you're only vaguely interested in.

Anyway. Apps off phone. Desktop only. It works.

Same principle applies to any retail app. Clothing stores. Home goods. That app for the bookstore you love. That app for the art supply store even though you haven't painted in six months. Delete all of them.

You're probably thinking: "But I actually need some of those apps for legitimate purchases."

Do you, though?

When was the last time you needed to make a purchase so urgently that you couldn't wait until you were at a computer? I'm not talking about ordering food or getting a ride. I mean retail purchases. The things impulse spending happens around.

If you genuinely need something, you can access the website from a browser. The extra thirty seconds it takes to navigate there instead of tapping an app icon is enough to give your prefrontal cortex time to wake up and ask whether this is actually a good idea.

Let's talk about browser extensions for a second, because there are some genuinely useful tools that can help with this.

There's an extension—several, actually, but they all work roughly the same way—that blocks specific websites or limits your time on them. You can set it so Amazon is blocked after 9 PM. Or so you can only access it for fifteen minutes per day. Or so it's completely blocked except for a list of specific times you've pre-scheduled.

Sounds extreme, maybe. But remember: you're not fighting fair. These platforms have literal teams of PhDs in behavioral psychology working full-time to make their sites as addictive as possible. You're one person with a limited amount of willpower trying to make good decisions while tired. The game is rigged. Blocking software evens the odds.

Another option: extensions that remove the parts of websites specifically designed to trigger impulse purchases.

There's one that hides the "recommended for you" section on Amazon. Another that removes suggested videos from YouTube (different problem, same principle—algorithmic recommendations designed to keep you engaged longer than you intended). Another that strips ads from websites entirely.

You can also use browser extensions that add friction in other ways. One I've seen forces you to wait thirty seconds before completing a purchase. Just thirty seconds of a timer counting down before the "confirm order" button becomes clickable.

Sounds like nothing, right? But a lot of impulse purchases happen in that instant-gratification window where you don't want to think about it, you just want it done. Thirty seconds is enough time for the impulse to fade. For your brain to go "wait, do I actually need this, or am I just buying it because I'm bored?"

Another one makes you type out "I want to buy this" before you can add something to your cart. Sounds silly. Works surprisingly well. Something about having to consciously articulate the action makes it feel less automatic.

The point isn't to make shopping impossible. It's to make it *deliberate*. To insert just enough pause into the process that you're making an actual choice instead of running a program your brain learned six months ago when you were stressed about something completely unrelated.

Now let's talk about phone settings, because your phone is probably the single biggest source of spending cues in your life.

Notifications are the obvious one. Every time your phone buzzes with a promotional message or a sale alert or a "we miss you" email from some store you shopped at once eight months ago, that's a cue. A little nudge toward the shopping behavior.

Turn them all off.

Not just mute. Off. Go into settings for every single retail app (before you delete them, which you're also doing) and disable notifications. Then go into your email settings and turn off notifications for promotional emails. Or—better option—set up a filter that automatically sorts promotional emails into a separate folder that you only check when you're specifically looking for something.

Your phone should not be pinging you with opportunities to spend money. That's not what it's for. Or at least, that's not what it should be for in a world where you're trying to control impulse spending.

But notifications are just the surface level. The deeper issue is how accessible your phone makes shopping in general.

There's a setting on most phones now—Screen Time on iPhone, Digital Wellbeing on Android—that lets you see exactly how much time you spend in each app and set limits. Go look at yours right now. I'll wait.

Look at how much time you're spending in shopping apps, or in browsers visiting retail sites, or in social media apps that are mostly just ad delivery systems with some content sprinkled in between.

Add it up. How many hours per week are you spending in environments specifically designed to make you want to buy things?

Now set limits. Tell your phone you only get thirty minutes per day on Instagram. Or an hour per week on shopping sites. When you hit the limit, the app locks. You can override it if you really need to—it's not a jail, it's a speed bump—but you have to actively choose to override it, which again, breaks the autopilot pattern.

You can also set downtime schedules. Phone goes into "do not disturb" mode after 9 PM, and certain apps just aren't accessible until morning.

Is this all starting to sound a little controlling? A little like you're treating yourself like a teenager who can't be trusted with their own phone?

Yeah. It kind of is.

But here's the thing: your teenager self—the impulsive part of your brain that wants immediate gratification and doesn't think about consequences—is the part that's making spending decisions when you're tired or stressed or bored. Your adult self, the part that actually cares about your financial goals, needs to set up boundaries ahead of time so teenage-you doesn't blow the budget on stuff you don't need.

You're not punishing yourself. You're protecting future-you from the decisions past-you tends to make in low moments.

Physical environment matters too, by the way. Not just digital.

If you work from home and you're vulnerable to browsing shopping sites when you're procrastinating on work stuff (which, let's be honest, most of us are), change where you work. Move your laptop to a different room. Face your desk toward a window instead of a wall. Put your phone in a drawer across the room instead of on the desk next to you.

The goal is to make the path from "I'm frustrated with this task" to "I'm browsing products I don't need" just a little bit longer. A little less automatic.

If you tend to shop while watching TV in the evening, try keeping your phone in a different room during TV time. Or put it in one of those timed lock boxes—yeah, they make those, little safes where you set a timer and it won't open until the timer's done. Sounds extreme. Also works.

Or just charge your phone in the bathroom instead of on your nightstand. So if you want to browse before bed, you have to get up and go get it. Which you probably won't do, because you're already comfortable and getting up sounds like work.

These all sound like tiny changes. They are tiny changes. That's the point.

You're not trying to become a completely different person with ironclad discipline. You're trying to add small amounts of friction to the specific pathways your impulses tend to follow.

Let's talk about what to do with the time you get back, because that matters more than you'd think.

If you're spending, say, forty-five minutes a day scrolling through shopping sites or Instagram ads or browsing stuff you don't need, and you successfully block all of that, you suddenly have forty-five minutes of empty space in your day.

Your brain is going to want to fill that space with *something*. If you don't give it something, it'll default back to the old behavior. The path is already carved. It's easy. It's right there.

So you need a replacement behavior ready.

What else gives you that same hit of novelty or excitement or temporary relief from boredom that shopping was providing?

For some people, it's reading. Actual books, or articles, or longform stuff they've been saving but never getting to. For some people, it's cooking, or going for a walk, or calling a friend they haven't talked to in a while.

The replacement doesn't have to be productive. It doesn't have to improve you or make you a better person. It just has to be something you genuinely enjoy that doesn't cost money every time you do it.

I know someone who replaced late-night shopping with playing old video games she already owned. Another person started doing jigsaw puzzles. Another person got really into watching YouTube videos about how things are made—like, factory tours and manufacturing processes. None of these are going to change your life. They're just pleasant ways to occupy your brain that don't involve adding things to a cart.

The point is to have *something* ready for when the urge hits. Because the urge will hit. You're not eliminating the emotional need. You're redirecting it.

Think of it like this: you're a river. For a long time, you've been flowing toward shopping. You've carved a canyon in that direction. The water wants to go there. It's the path of least resistance.

You're trying to redirect the river.

But you can't just build a dam and expect the water to stop flowing. It has to go somewhere. So you dig a new channel. You make it easy for the water to flow in a different direction. And over time, the new path becomes automatic too.

One more thing, and this one might be the hardest to hear: you probably need to have some hard conversations with the people in your life.

If you have a friend who constantly sends you links to products with "OMG you need this," that's a cue. A direct invitation to shop. And if you're trying to reduce impulse spending, that's working against you.

You don't have to cut the friend out of your life, obviously. But you might need to say something like: "Hey, I'm trying to be more intentional about spending, so I'd appreciate it if you didn't send me shopping links for a while."

Most people will get it. Some won't. Some will take it personally, or think you're being dramatic, or "forget" and keep sending you links anyway.

That tells you something useful about the relationship, honestly. But that's a different book.

Same goes for family dynamics around gift-giving. If your love language is gifts and you express affection by buying people things, and you're trying to cut back on spending, you need to find a different way to show you care. Which is uncomfortable! It feels like you're losing a tool. But that tool is expensive, and it's not actually serving you as well as you think it is.

Or if you have a family culture where everyone's constantly talking about their latest purchases, comparing deals, showing off new stuff—that environment is actively working against your goals. Every conversation is a cue. A reminder that shopping is how people in your circle bond and communicate status and spend their free time.

You might need to extract yourself from some of those conversations. Or redirect them. Or just be honest: "I'm trying not to think about shopping right now, can we talk about something else?"

Will it be awkward? Yes. Will some people think you're being weird or preachy or annoying? Probably.

But the alternative is staying in an environment that constantly triggers the behavior you're trying to change, and then wondering why your willpower keeps failing.

Your willpower isn't failing. Your environment is too strong.

Here's what I want you to take away from all of this: you are not broken.

The system is designed to make you spend impulsively. The apps, the websites, the algorithms, the email campaigns, the influencers, the ads disguised as content, all of it. Billions of dollars have been spent figuring out exactly how to bypass your conscious decision-making and trigger automatic behaviors that end with you clicking "buy now."

You're not failing because you lack discipline. You're failing because you're trying to resist a system that's designed by experts to be irresistible, and you're doing it alone, with limited resources, at the end of a long day when you're tired and your defenses are down.

The answer isn't to try harder. It's to change the battlefield.

Remove the cues. Add friction. Replace the behavior. Redesign your environment so the path of least resistance leads somewhere other than shopping.

It won't be perfect. You'll still have impulses. You'll still occasionally buy things you don't need. That's fine. You're human. The goal isn't perfection. The goal is to break the *automatic* nature of it. To turn impulse spending from an unconscious pattern into a conscious choice you make sometimes, in specific circumstances, for specific reasons.

And once it's a choice? You're back in control.

Not because you got stronger. Because you got smarter about how your brain works and what it needs and how to design around its weaknesses instead of just trying to power through them.

Which, honestly, is harder in some ways. Because it requires you to actually look at your patterns and admit that the current setup isn't working and make changes that feel uncomfortable at first.

But here's what happens when you do that work: shopping stops being this constant background hum of temptation that you're always half-resisting. It becomes something you do intentionally, when you've decided it serves you, instead of something that happens *to* you while you're thinking about other things.

And that shift—from passive to active, from autopilot to intentional—is where everything changes.

Not all at once. Not dramatically. But somewhere in the next few weeks, you'll have a moment where you feel the urge to buy something, and instead of immediately opening an app or a website, you'll pause. You'll notice the urge. You'll recognize it as a response to being tired or stressed or bored. And you'll choose something else.

Maybe you'll go for a walk. Maybe you'll text a friend. Maybe you'll just sit with the feeling for thirty seconds until it passes.

And it will pass. The urge, I mean. They always do, if you give them a minute.

That first time you successfully notice an impulse and choose not to act on it? That's not you being stronger. That's you having successfully redesigned your environment so the impulse has nowhere to go.

And the second time it happens, it'll be a little easier. And the third time, easier still.

Not because the impulses get weaker—they might, over time, but that's not the mechanism here—but because you've built a new set of pathways. New channels for the river to flow through.

That's what we're building toward. One small design change at a time.

Sarah deleted Instagram on Tuesday. By Thursday she'd reinstalled it 'just to check something.' The cue got through anyway.

Chapter 6: Sarah's First Month: A Real-Life Test

The scented candle arrived on a Thursday. Sarah doesn't remember ordering it—not the decision part, anyway. Just the clicking. Late Tuesday night, supposed to be finishing a client project, saw the candle, clicked. 'Woodland Berry.' Thirty-two dollars. When she opened the package, she felt nothing. Not joy. Not satisfaction. Just faint embarrassment.

Sarah's candle isn't my sister's handbag—it's cheaper, less useful, and she didn't even remember wanting it. But both of them are symptoms of the same thing: trying to survive a system built on deprivation.

She set it on her desk next to the other candle she'd impulse-bought two weeks earlier (still in its packaging), and the decorative succulent from the month before that (already dying because she kept forgetting to water it), and the set of gel pens she'd never used. A little graveyard of things that were supposed to make her feel better and didn't.

That candle is still sitting there, by the way. I asked her about it months later, and she laughed—a slightly bitter laugh—and said she'd finally lit it once, hated the smell, and threw it out. Thirty-two dollars for an experience that lasted approximately four minutes. She told me she thought about that candle a lot during her first month trying to change her spending habits. Not because it was the worst purchase she'd ever made, but because it was so *perfectly representative* of the problem.

Here's what I want you to understand about Sarah before we go any further: she's not reckless. She's not living beyond her means in any dramatic sense. She's a thirty-two-year-old graphic designer who works remotely, makes a decent living—around $4,800 a month after taxes and health insurance—and pays her bills on time. Her rent is $1,600, utilities run about $250, internet is $75, car payment and insurance together come to around $500. She even contributes $400 monthly to her 401k, which is more than a lot of people her age manage.

On paper, she's doing fine.

But here's the thing nobody tells you about "doing fine": it can coexist with a low-grade financial anxiety that never quite goes away. Sarah had that anxiety. The kind that lives in your chest and whispers at you every time you check your bank balance. The kind that makes you avoid looking at your credit card statement for a few extra days because you already know it's going to be higher than you planned.

When she finally sat down and tracked her spending—really tracked it, every single transaction for a month—she discovered she was hemorrhaging between $500 and $600 monthly on what she diplomatically called "unplanned purchases." Books she didn't read. Clothes she wore once. Online courses she enrolled in during bursts of optimism and abandoned after the first video. Mugs. God, so many mugs. She counted them one afternoon and found fourteen novelty mugs in her cupboard, each one purchased in a moment of "this will make my morning coffee more enjoyable" delusion.

You're probably thinking: well, if she knows she's spending $600 a month on nonsense, why doesn't she just...stop?

And look, I get it. From the outside, the solution seems obvious. Stop buying things you don't need. Exercise some discipline. Just don't click the button. But if you've ever tried to "just stop" an ingrained habit—and I'm guessing you have, or you wouldn't be reading this book—you know it's not that simple. Sarah knew intellectually that she should stop. She'd given herself that lecture dozens of times. It never worked for more than a few days.

Because here's what was actually happening: Sarah worked from home, often alone for eight or nine hours a day. The isolation got to her. Not in a dramatic, crushing way—more like a constant background hum of loneliness that she'd learned to tune out most of the time. But when the hum got louder—when she'd been staring at her screen for three hours straight, or when a project wasn't going well, or when she felt that particular brand of restless boredom that comes from too much solitude—she'd open a browser tab. Just to look. Just to browse.

Except "just browsing" doesn't really exist anymore, does it? The algorithms know when you're vulnerable. They know when you're bored, when you're tired, when your defenses are down. So they show you the thing. The perfectly styled desk setup that would definitely make you more productive. The sweater that looks exactly like the one that celebrity wore in that photo you saw yesterday. The cookbook that will absolutely transform you into the kind of person who makes elaborate weeknight dinners instead of eating cereal over the sink.

And the promise embedded in each of these things is so seductive: *This will fix something. This will make you feel better.*

For Sarah, the actual moment of purchase—the clicking, the entering of credit card details, the confirmation email—felt good. A little spike of dopamine, a sense of having done something, taken action, moved forward. It was only later, when the package arrived or the charge appeared on her statement, that the regret set in. But by then she was already halfway to the next purchase.

This is the cycle we talked about earlier in the book, but I want you to see what it looks like in real time, in a real person's life. Because Sarah isn't a cautionary tale. She's probably a lot like you. (She's definitely a lot like I was, before I figured out how much of my "financial personality" was actually just unexamined habit.)

So when Sarah decided to try the system—the friction-based, fun-money-account approach we've been building through this book—she wasn't coming in as a blank slate. She was coming in with years of conditioning, with deeply grooved neural pathways that connected "bored" to "browse" to "buy." The first month wasn't about perfection. It was about interrupting those pathways enough times that they started to weaken.

Let me show you what that looked like.

Week one was disorienting. That's the word she used when we talked about it: disorienting. She'd set up her fun money account—she started with $150, which felt simultaneously generous and restrictive—and implemented the 24-hour delay rule for anything over $20. The first time an impulse hit, she did what she was supposed to: added the item (a set of watercolor paints she'd probably never use) to her "wait list" on her phone and closed the browser.

Then she just...sat there. Feeling weird.

Because the transaction had always been the resolution. The wanting led to the buying, and the buying ended the wanting. Now the wanting just kind of...hung there. She described it as being uncomfortably aware of the desire without being able to satisfy it immediately, like suddenly noticing your own breathing and not being able to make it feel automatic again.

She almost gave up the whole system on day three. She'd had a frustrating morning—a client kept requesting revisions that contradicted their earlier feedback, that special kind of work torture—and her brain was *screaming* for relief. She found herself on a clothing website without consciously deciding to go there, hovering over a cardigan that was on sale.

Here's what she told me: "I could feel the justification building. It's on sale. I need a new cardigan anyway. It's only forty dollars. And I remember thinking, *this is stupid, why am I making myself wait, I'm a grown woman with money in my bank account, I should be able to buy a cardigan if I want one.*"

But—and this is the crucial part—she'd told me she was going to try the system for at least two weeks. She'd said it out loud to another person. So even though every fiber of her wanted to just buy the damn cardigan, she added it to the wait list. Then she closed her laptop, walked to her kitchen, and stress-ate half a bag of chips while standing at the counter.

Not exactly a triumph of willpower. But not a purchase, either.

Twenty-four hours later, she looked at the cardigan again. Still liked it. Still wanted it. But the *urgency* had evaporated. It was just a cardigan now, not a solution to her emotional state. She thought about it for another day, checked her fun money balance ($150, untouched), and bought it. Forty dollars. Well within her budget. And when it arrived, she actually wore it regularly—because she'd wanted the cardigan itself, not the feeling of purchasing something.

That's the first thing she learned: the 24-hour delay didn't eliminate her wants. It just separated the real ones from the emotional self-medication.

By the end of week one, she'd used $60 from her fun money account. The cardigan, a book she'd been eyeing for weeks, and an expensive coffee drink that she purchased deliberately, on a Saturday afternoon, as a treat rather than a reflex. She still had $90 left for the month. That felt...good? Strange, but good.

Week two is when she started noticing the patterns.

She'd heard me talk about triggers—how impulse spending usually isn't random, it clusters around specific emotional states or times of day—but she hadn't really believed it applied to her. She thought her shopping was more scattered, more opportunistic. But when she started actually paying attention, the pattern was embarrassingly obvious.

Late afternoon. Specifically between 3:00 and 4:30 PM. That's when the work day started dragging, when her focus would slip, when she'd tell herself she deserved a "little break" that inevitably turned into twenty minutes of online browsing. The lighting in her apartment shifted at that time too—the sun moved behind the building across the street, and her workspace got dimmer and somehow more depressing. She'd never connected these things before. Now she couldn't unsee the connection.

She tried something that felt almost laughably simple: at 3:00 PM, before the urge hit, she'd take an actual break. Not a "scroll through my phone" break. She'd stand up, do some stretches, sometimes walk around the block, sometimes just stand on her balcony for five minutes. Preemptive strike against the boredom.

It worked maybe half the time. The other half, she'd still feel the pull toward shopping sites. But even when she did browse, she was *aware* she was doing it as a response to a specific feeling, and that awareness created just enough distance to keep her from buying most of the time.

The other pattern she noticed: social media. Instagram specifically. She'd known intellectually that ads were designed to manipulate her, but she hadn't fully reckoned with how *effective* they were. A well-targeted ad could create a want she didn't have thirty seconds earlier. It was like watching someone plant a thought in her head in real time.

She tried cutting back her Instagram use and made it about two days before she gave up—she genuinely enjoyed parts of the app, and going cold turkey felt unnecessarily punitive. Instead, she made a rule: if she felt the impulse to buy something she'd seen on Instagram, she had to wait 48 hours instead of 24. Just because.

This turned out to be remarkably effective, because Instagram-fueled wants were almost always the most fleeting. The algorithm was very good at creating desire, but that desire was weirdly fragile. It couldn't survive two days of inattention.

One night during week two, she slipped up. Not dramatically—she didn't blow her whole budget or anything—but she bought a phone case she didn't need because she was feeling anxious about an upcoming project deadline and wanted something to look forward to. It was $18, which felt small enough that she almost didn't count it as breaking the rules. But then she felt terrible about it, that familiar wash of guilt and disappointment in herself.

Here's what I told her, and what I want to tell you: slip-ups aren't failures. They're data. Sarah had just learned that project anxiety was another trigger. She'd also learned that she was still capable of using shopping as an emotional pacifier when the stress got high enough.

This wasn't a character flaw. It was information she could use.

The phone case arrived four days later. She looked at it, felt nothing, and gave it to her sister.

By week three, something had shifted. She still felt impulses—they didn't magically disappear—but they'd lost some of their power. Or maybe she'd gained power over them; I'm not sure the distinction matters.

She found herself thinking about the *why* more. Not in a judgmental way, but genuinely curious. When she wanted to buy something, she'd pause and ask: what do I actually want right now? Sometimes the answer was "I want that specific jacket." But more often, the answer was something like "I want to feel like I'm treating myself well" or "I want a distraction from this boring task" or "I want to feel like I have my life together, and people who have their lives together own aesthetically pleasing desk organizers."

Once she named the underlying want, it became easier to address it directly. Feeling like she needed to treat herself? She'd make her favorite pasta for dinner, or watch an episode of the show she was saving. Needing a distraction? Five-minute break, away from screens. Wanting to feel put-together? Sometimes that actually *did* mean buying something—but now she was making that choice consciously, from the fun money account, rather than reflexively.

The fun money account itself had become strangely liberating. She'd worried it would feel restrictive, like an allowance. Instead, it felt like permission. She had $150 a month that was *for* enjoying herself, no guilt required. As long as she stayed within that boundary, she could spend it on whatever brought her genuine pleasure.

And weirdly, knowing she *could* spend it made her less likely to spend it impulsively. She started curating more carefully. She'd see something she liked, add it to the list, and then think: is this really how I want to use my fun money this month? Sometimes yes. Often no. She started prioritizing experiences over objects—a nice dinner with friends, a pottery class she'd been curious about, concert tickets. These felt more satisfying, left less clutter in her apartment, and aligned better with the kind of life she actually wanted to live.

She told me something during week three that stuck with me. She said: "I think I've been buying things to prove to myself that I can. Like, I make decent money now—I grew up pretty broke, and there's still this part of me that gets a rush from being able to afford things. But I'm starting to realize that the better proof isn't buying whatever I want. It's choosing not to buy things and feeling secure anyway."

I think about that a lot. The idea that for some of us, impulse spending isn't really about the items at all. It's about trying to feel secure, or abundant, or like we've made it. And the trap is that the buying actually undermines that feeling—because you end up with less money, less control, more anxiety about your finances.

Real abundance, it turns out, might look more like having money left over. Like knowing you could buy something and choosing not to. Like curating your life intentionally instead of just accumulating.

Week four, Sarah did something I hadn't suggested: she started tracking not just what she bought, but what she *almost* bought and didn't. She kept a note on her phone with every item she'd added to the wait list and then ultimately passed on.

By the end of the month, the list was staggering. Thirty-seven items. She added up what they would have cost: $847.

She'd spent $130 of her $150 fun money budget—the cardigan, a couple of books, concert tickets, a nice dinner. She'd enjoyed all of it. None of it had triggered that familiar buyer's remorse. And she'd avoided spending $847 on things she didn't actually want.

But here's what she said was the biggest change, and I believe her: she felt calmer. The low-grade financial anxiety that had been humming in the background for years—that feeling of never quite knowing where her money was going, never quite feeling in control—had quieted significantly. Not gone entirely, but manageable. She wasn't white-knuckling her way through temptation. She was just...making different choices.

She'd also become aware of how much mental energy she'd been devoting to shopping. The browsing, the comparing prices, the justifying purchases, the mild guilt afterward. All of that had been taking up space in her brain. Now that space was freed up for other things—her work, her hobbies, her relationships, actual relaxation instead of the fake relaxation of scrolling through shopping sites.

At the end of the month, she transferred the remaining $20 from her fun money account to her savings goal: the house down payment fund. It wasn't a huge amount, but it was something. More importantly, she'd proven to herself that the system worked. That she could enjoy her life, spend money on things that mattered to her, and still make progress toward her long-term goals.

She wasn't "cured" of impulse spending. That's not how habits work. She still felt tempted sometimes. But she had a framework now, a set of tools that helped her navigate those impulses without being controlled by them.

I want to be honest with you about something. When I first started developing this system—the friction techniques, the fun money account, all of it—I thought it was primarily a tactical solution to a tactical problem. You want to spend less impulsively? Here's how to make that harder.

But watching Sarah's first month, and talking to her about what was actually happening internally, I realized I'd been wrong about what the system was really doing. Yes, it was creating friction and providing structure. But more fundamentally, it was giving her a way to be deliberate instead of reactive. It was teaching her that she could feel a desire without immediately acting on it. That she could sit with discomfort—boredom, anxiety, restlessness—without needing to buy something to make it go away.

That's not really about money. It's about autonomy. About being the person who decides what you do, rather than being yanked around by whatever impulse happens to be loudest at the moment.

Sarah's working on month two now. She told me last week that she's thinking about increasing her fun money budget to $200—not because she's struggling to stay within $150, but because she wants more room to save up for bigger experiences she's excited about. A weekend trip. A really good piece of art for her apartment. Things that require patience and planning, that she'll appreciate more because she chose them deliberately.

And she's started noticing something else, something I find particularly interesting: the items she does buy now, she values more. They're not just things she owns; they're things she chose. There's a difference. When you've given yourself space to consider whether you really want something, and you decide you do, and you purchase it intentionally from money you've specifically allocated for that purpose—the object carries more meaning. It's not just clutter. It's a deliberate part of your life.

That $40 cardigan? She wears it constantly. It's become her favorite piece of clothing, not because it's objectively superior to anything else in her closet, but because buying it was a *choice* rather than a reflex.

The Woodland Berry candle, on the other hand—the one that started this whole chapter—is gone now, thrown away after one disappointing use. But in a way, it served a purpose. It became a symbol for her of the old pattern, the one where she'd buy things to fill some unnamed lack and then wonder why she still felt empty.

She doesn't do that anymore. Not never—let's be realistic—but not as the default. And that shift, more than any specific dollar amount saved, is what's actually changed her relationship with money.

She's building something now. Not just a down payment fund, though that's growing steadily. She's building the capacity to choose the life she wants rather than defaulting to whatever her impulses suggest in any given moment. That's harder than it sounds. It's also more valuable than most of what she used to buy.

The question she's sitting with now—the one she asked me last week, and the one I think you might be asking too—is this: if the system works, if she can see the progress, if she's feeling more in control and less anxious...what happens when the novelty wears off? When the tricks stop feeling effective because they've become familiar? When she hits a period of real stress or disruption and all the old patterns come roaring back?

The Woodland Berry candle is still on Sarah's desk. Burned about halfway down. She uses it sometimes. That's not the problem. The problem was that on Day 32, nothing felt different at all.

Chapter 7: Redirecting the Urge: The 'Pause & Plan' Script

I'm standing in Target at 9:47 PM on a Wednesday holding a throw pillow I have no reason to own. Cream-colored. Little tufted spots that look like clouds. Twenty-four ninety-nine. My couch already has four pillows. The detergent I came for is already in my cart. I could leave right now. But I'm still standing here.

It's cream-colored with little tufted spots that look like clouds, and it costs $24.99, and I have absolutely no reason to own it. My couch already has four pillows. I came here for laundry detergent. The detergent is in my cart. I could leave right now, go home, do my laundry, and my life would be completely fine.

But I'm not leaving. I'm standing here, running my thumb over the tufted spots, imagining how it would look on my couch (good, obviously—Target's visual merchandising team knows exactly what they're doing), and constructing an elaborate internal defense. It would brighten up the living room. It's practically on sale—$24.99 feels like it should be marked down from something higher, right? I work hard. Don't I deserve a throw pillow?

Here's what I'm not thinking about: the fact that I bought a different throw pillow three weeks ago. Or that I'm trying to save for a new phone. Or that "I work hard" and "I deserve this" is the exact justification I used for the scented candle last week, the face serum the week before that, and the organizational baskets still in their packaging.

I'm not thinking about any of that because impulse spending isn't really about thinking. It's about a very old part of my brain—the part that evolved to grab the ripe fruit before someone else does—completely overriding the part that plans and budgets and remembers I already have four pillows.

And that's not a personal failing. That's just being human in an environment specifically designed to exploit being human.

Amazon's algorithms predict what you'll buy before you know you want it. Instagram serves you ads based on things you didn't even realize you'd paused to look at. That sale timer counting down ("Only 3 left in stock!") is engineered to trigger your scarcity response—the same response that kept your ancestors alive during famines, now repurposed to sell you supplements you'll take twice and forget about.

We're biological organisms with stone-age wiring trying to navigate a commercial environment that's evolved faster in the last twenty years than we have in the last two hundred thousand. And we're supposed to just... have better willpower?

I put down the pillow that night because I'd started using a specific script—a set of steps I could follow when my rational brain had already logged off for the day. I'm going to teach you that script in this chapter. But first you need to understand why it works, and why everything you've probably tried before hasn't.

Most impulse-control advice assumes that if you just *knew better*, you'd *do better*. If you understood compound interest, you wouldn't buy the latte. If you really grasped the importance of emergency funds, you'd stop shopping online at midnight.

But you do know better. You know exactly how compound interest works. You know you need an emergency fund. You know buying stuff doesn't actually make you happier beyond the five minutes of unboxing it.

Knowing doesn't stop the impulse. Because the impulse isn't happening in the knowing part of your brain.

It's happening in the part that's reaching for relief from boredom, or stress, or loneliness, or that vague sense of lack that modern life generates constantly. Shopping—especially online shopping—is the fastest, easiest culturally-acceptable way to get that relief. It's legal, it's private, it requires no skill, and it works. Briefly. Until the package arrives and you feel nothing, or worse, you feel guilty, and then you need another hit.

So we need a different strategy. Not more information. Not more shame. A circuit breaker. Something that interrupts the automatic loop between "I want that" and "I just bought that" and creates enough space for you to actually choose.

That's the Pause & Plan script. Three steps, genuinely simple—but simple doesn't mean easy. Think of it less like a magic spell and more like a fire extinguisher. You still have to use it when the fire starts. But once you know where it is and how it works, you've got a fighting chance.

Let me show you how I learned this. We're going back to Powell's Books in Portland, five years ago—my least favorite memory of my own financial dysfunction and the thing that finally snapped me out of it.

I had a book problem. Not a reading problem—a *buying* books problem. I could not walk into a bookstore without walking out with a stack. Three books minimum, usually closer to six or seven. I'd go in with a specific title in mind and somehow end up at the register with an armful of things I'd convinced myself I needed.

The rationalizations were beautiful. Intricate. Airtight. These were *investments* in my education (I'm a financial coach—surely reading about behavioral economics makes me better at my job?). I was *supporting* independent bookstores. Hardcovers were *worth* the extra money because they'd last longer (never mind that I had two hundred unread books at home, many still in their shrink wrap).

Every justification was technically true and completely irrelevant to the actual problem: I was spending $300 a month on books I would never read while simultaneously being unable to afford new windshield wipers. Or a trip to visit my sister. Or literally any financial cushion against disaster.

But I didn't see it as a problem. I saw it as a personality trait. "I'm just a book person! I love books! You can't put a price on knowledge!"

(You absolutely can put a price on knowledge. It's usually printed right on the back cover.)

The turning point: Powell's, business section, early evening. Three books in my hands. One on habit formation, one on systems thinking, one on economic history—I think. I genuinely don't remember, which should tell you something. I'm standing there, already mentally committed to buying them, already imagining how smart I'll feel reading them.

Then I looked at my phone to check the time and saw my bank balance notification.

$180 in checking. Rent was paid. But that was it. One hundred eighty dollars to last until the next paycheck, eight days away. And I was about to spend $60 of it on books.

For the first time—maybe ever—I actually let myself connect those two facts. $60 on books meant $120 for eight days. Meant skipping the birthday dinner I'd told my friend I'd go to. Meant saying no to coffee with my sister when she visited. Meant another week of that low-grade anxiety that comes from knowing you're one unexpected expense away from overdrafting.

And for what? Three books I probably wouldn't read for six months, if ever. Three books I wouldn't even remember buying by next Tuesday.

I put them down. Just set them on the nearest table and walked out.

Felt absolutely *awful* doing it. Not virtuous. Not proud. Felt like I was denying myself something essential, like I was being stingy and joyless. My brain was throwing a full tantrum. "You *need* these. You'll regret not buying them. Someone else will get them. You work hard; you deserve nice things. They're *books*, not frivolous garbage; this is *self-improvement*."

The voice was so loud I almost turned around three times on the walk back to my car.

But I didn't. And here's what shocked me: by the time I got home, twenty minutes later, I'd completely forgotten which books they were.

Gone. The intense, urgent *need* I'd felt in the store had evaporated. I could remember the *feeling*—the wanting, the imagining, the little dopamine spike of anticipation—but I could not remember the actual books.

I went back through my credit card statements from the previous six months. I remembered almost none of it. I remembered the *act* of buying—walking to the register, the satisfaction of the transaction, the weight of the bag. But the actual books? Blank.

That's when I realized: I wasn't buying books. I was buying the *feeling* of buying books. And the feeling lasted about as long as it took to get to my car.

So I started building the script. Not all at once—more like I noticed what had worked at Powell's (stopping, creating space, asking myself a real question) and started trying to replicate it.

Here's what it became:

Step one: Pause. Physically interrupt the momentum.

If you're online: close the tab. If you're in a store: put the item down. If someone's pressuring you—salespeople are *extremely* good at creating artificial urgency—say "I need a minute to think" and walk away. Even if it feels rude. Especially if they're giving you a look, because that look is part of the sales tactic.

This step sounds trivial. It is not. Your brain will fight you *hard*. It'll tell you you're overthinking, you're being silly, you'll miss the deal, you'll regret it, just buy it already.

That voice is very convincing. It is neither urgent nor true. It's just your dopamine system lobbying for the quick hit.

Ignore it. Sixty seconds. That's all you need.

Here's the trick I use: I imagine the thing is already gone. Sold out. Someone else bought the last one. How do I feel?

If the answer is devastated—genuinely upset, not just momentarily disappointed—okay, maybe this is something I actually want. But if there's even a flicker of *relief*? That's the real answer. That's your actual self trying to get a word in while the impulse part is shouting.

Take three slow breaths. (I know. I *know* how that sounds. But it works for an extremely boring, non-spiritual reason: deep breathing activates your parasympathetic nervous system, which calms the fight-or-flight response that impulse spending actually triggers. You're not meditating. You're hacking your biology so the planning part of your brain can boot back up.)

Step two: Ask the trade-off question. Make the cost concrete.

Not "Can I afford this?"—that question is too abstract when you're already emotionally invested. Not "Do I need this?"—because you obviously don't *need* the throw pillow, and "need" is way too easy to argue with.

The question that actually works: **"If I buy this, what am I not buying?"**

Money is finite. Every dollar you spend here is a dollar you don't have for something else. What is that something else? Be specific. Don't let yourself off with vague answers like "future stuff" or "I'll figure it out later."

I keep a list on my phone—things I'm actively saving for. Not abstract someday-goals like "retirement." Concrete things that would genuinely upset me to delay or sacrifice.

Right now mine says: new tires for my car (I've been pushing this way too long), plane tickets to see my sister in August, and a replacement for my laptop, which is making ominous clicking sounds and probably has six months left.

When I'm tempted to buy something, I pull up that list. Suddenly the choice isn't "buy this or be a joyless miser." It's "buy this *instead of* new tires." Or "buy this and push the laptop replacement into next year."

That reframe—from deprivation to trade-off—changes everything. You're not being virtuous or disciplined. You're just choosing. Like choosing between two things on a menu.

Most of the time, when I make it concrete like that, the impulse item loses. Not because I've shamed myself out of wanting it. Because I want the other thing more. I want the relief of having new tires more than I want the candle. I want to see my sister more than I want the decorative basket.

Sometimes, though? The impulse item wins. And that's fine. If I genuinely want the $35 face serum more than I want to put $35 toward my laptop fund this week, I can make that choice consciously. The script isn't about never spending money on fun things. It's about making sure I'm *choosing*, not just reacting.

Step three: Plan the replacement. Redirect the need.

This is the step most advice skips. It's why most advice fails.

You can't just suppress an urge. Doesn't work. The urge will pop back up an hour later, or tomorrow, louder and more insistent.

You have to redirect it.

The impulse is usually pointing at something real. You're not broken for wanting stuff. You're trying to meet a need—comfort, excitement, novelty, a sense of control, connection, *something*—and spending money is the fastest, easiest, most culturally-normalized way we have to do that. It works. Briefly.

So if you don't buy the thing, you still need to address the actual need underneath. Otherwise you're just white-knuckling through the moment, which is exhausting and not sustainable.

What do you actually need right now?

Bored? Call someone. Go for a walk. Rearrange a room. Do that project you've been avoiding. Play a game you already own. Read one of the seventeen unread books on your shelf.

Stressed? Move your body. Any movement. Dance in your kitchen. Do ten jumping jacks. Stretch on the floor. Physical movement disrupts the stress response faster than almost anything else, and it costs zero dollars.

Sad or lonely? Reach out to someone. Text a friend. Call your mom (if calling your mom doesn't make you more sad—know your own context). Join an online community about something you care about. The impulse to spend when you're sad is almost always a disguised need for connection or comfort, and buying things delivers neither. Not really. Not in any way that lasts past the unboxing.

Excited and want to celebrate? Find a way to honor that without spending. Make your favorite meal. Take yourself somewhere you've never been—in your own city. Create something. The goal is to *match* the energy of the feeling, not squash it.

I have a second list on my phone: things I can do instead of spending. Not virtuous, character-building activities. Things I actually *enjoy*. Things that meet the real needs my impulse spending is usually trying to address.

Mine right now: calling my friend Allie (we can talk for two hours without noticing). Playing guitar (badly—I'm extremely mediocre, but it's fun and I don't have to be good at fun things). Going to the park near my house that has excellent dog-watching. Reorganizing my bookshelves. Making elaborate breakfasts—I'm very good at pancakes and very bad at almost every other type of cooking, so breakfast is my moment to shine.

Your list will look completely different. That's the point. It has to be personal. It has to be full of things you genuinely want to do, not things you think you *should* want to do. If you hate exercising, don't put "go for a run" on the list. This only works if it's honest.

Make the list now, before you need it. Because in the moment, when the urge hits, your brain will go completely blank. You won't be able to think of a single thing you enjoy that doesn't cost money. Having it written down gives you something to grab onto.

Let me show you what this looks like in practice.

Last month. Spectacularly bad day. The kind where everything goes wrong starting at 7 AM—spilled coffee, missed an important email, back-to-back meetings with difficult clients, forgot to eat lunch, nearly got sideswiped in traffic—and by 8 PM I was fried.

I was on my couch, doomscrolling Instagram, and an ad popped up for this extremely cute jacket. Not even a jacket I needed—I own at least four already—but it was perfectly styled in the ad, and my exhausted brain went: "Yes. That. That will fix this day."

Before I fully registered what I was doing, I'd clicked through to the website, picked a size, picked a color, and was staring at a checkout screen for $180.

Old me—me from five years ago—would've just clicked "confirm" and dealt with the regret later. But I'd been using this script long enough that some part of me went: *Wait. Pause.*

I closed my laptop. Took three breaths. (Felt extremely silly. Did it anyway.)

Asked the trade-off question: If I spend $180 right now, what am I not buying?

Answer: I'm pushing back the trip to see my sister. Maybe to September. Maybe to October. Maybe not at all this year.

Did I want the jacket more than I wanted to see my sister?

Obviously not. But here's the insidious thing: in that moment, the jacket was *real*. It was right there, one click away. My sister was an abstraction. A future possibility. Not tangible.

So I made her tangible. Pulled up our last text conversation. Looked at photos from the last time I visited—us on her porch, talking until past midnight, the kind of conversation you can only have in person. Remembered what it felt like.

Then the choice was easy.

But I still had all this restless, frustrated energy from the bad day. The need the jacket had promised to meet—comfort, a sense of treating myself, *something nice* to counterbalance the garbage day—that was still there.

So I looked at my replacement list. Picked: make breakfast-for-dinner (scrambled eggs with about nine ingredients, fancy toast, the whole production), then call Allie.

By the time I'd finished cooking and eating and talking to Allie for ninety minutes, I felt better than I had all day. Genuinely better. Not the fake three-minute dopamine hit of clicking "buy now." Actually better.

And I never thought about the jacket again.

That's the script. Pause. Ask the trade-off question. Plan the replacement.

Three steps. Simple—not easy, but simple.

Will it work every single time? No. Sometimes you'll still buy the thing. Sometimes you'll be too tired or too stressed or too overwhelmed to catch yourself. That's fine. You're not trying to be perfect. You're trying to interrupt the automatic loop often enough that you actually get to choose instead of just react.

Start with one situation. Not all of them—that's too much. Pick the one that costs you the most, either in actual dollars or in guilt afterward. Online shopping at night? Impulse purchases at Target? Bookstores? (That was mine. Obviously.)

Use the script for that one situation. Get good at it there. Then expand.

Make your two lists: what you're saving for (the things you'd be upset to delay) and what you can do instead of spending (the things that meet the real needs). Keep them somewhere you'll actually see them when you need them. Your phone works. A note on your desk.

Wherever you usually are when the impulse hits.

And when it hits—when you're standing in Target at 9:47 PM holding a throw pillow you absolutely do not need, or staring at a checkout screen for something you'll forget about in twenty minutes—remember: you're not trying to develop superhuman willpower. You're just trying to give yourself sixty seconds of space between the wanting and the buying. Sixty seconds to choose.

That's all it takes.

I bought the pillow. I'm not going to pretend I didn't. I used the script, I paused, I planned—and then I bought it anyway. It's been on my couch for three years. I still like it. The script didn't fail. But it also didn't solve what came next.

Chapter 8: Beyond the First Month: Long-Term Maintenance

There's a Post-it note still stuck to my bathroom mirror from February 2019. 'Day 30' in green Sharpie, three exclamation points. I remember the feeling when I wrote it—like I'd crossed a finish line that actually mattered. The note's been there for seven years. Day 31, I bought a vintage typewriter on eBay.

I used to think of impulse spending as a leak I could patch: plug the hole, solve the problem. But that Post-it note on my mirror—'Day 30'—that was me thinking I'd patched it. Day 31 taught me the bucket itself was the problem.

The note's been there for seven years. I see it every morning when I brush my teeth. I never took it down because of what happened next.

Day 31, I bought a vintage typewriter on eBay. Seventy-five dollars. I'd never written anything that wasn't on a computer. Didn't matter. I wanted it with the kind of urgency that obliterates logic, and my brain helpfully reminded me that I'd been "so good" for a whole month, that I "deserved" something, that this was basically a reward for my discipline. The typewriter arrived, sat on a shelf for six months, and eventually went to Goodwill in a box with a manual I'd never opened.

That Post-it stayed up as a reminder: the first month isn't the finish line. It's the starting line for the actual work.

Most people never make it past Day 45. They do everything right for those first few weeks—track every impulse, run the script, watch their spending drop—and then something shifts. Not all at once. There's no dramatic failure, no single purchase that breaks the system. It's more like a slow leak in a tire. You don't notice it happening until you're already pulling over to the side of the road, wondering when everything went flat.

You're probably thinking I'm about to tell you that maintenance means eternal vigilance. That you'll need to track every purchase and question every impulse for the rest of your natural life, like some kind of financial monk who's transcended the desire for new things.

That's not where this is going.

The truth is weirder and more interesting: if you're still putting in the same level of effort at month six that you were at week one, you're doing something wrong. This isn't supposed to stay hard. The whole point is to build something that becomes automatic, that requires less conscious thought over time, not more.

But you can't skip steps. You can't force the automation. And you definitely can't treat that first successful month like you've solved the problem and now you can coast.

Let me show you what happens when you try.

Lisa runs a small marketing agency in Portland. She's the kind of person who color-codes her calendar and answers emails at 6 AM, which is why it surprised both of us when she couldn't figure out where $340 went in the first week of March.

She'd crushed February. I mean truly crushed it. Tracked every impulse, used her fun money account exactly as planned, ended the month $200 under her usual spending. She'd sent me a screenshot of her budget app with a row of green checkmarks, the kind of message that doesn't need words because the image says it all: *I did it. I figured this out.*

Then March happened. Or more accurately, March 4th happened—the day a client called to kill a project she'd been counting on, the same day her daughter got sent home from school with a stomach bug, the same day the dishwasher started making a grinding noise that definitely meant something expensive was wrong with it.

By March 7th, she'd stopped opening her budget app. By March 10th, she'd bought three different things online that she couldn't quite remember ordering. By March 15th, when we met for coffee and she finally looked at her account, she'd spent more in two weeks than she'd spent in the entire previous month.

"I don't understand what happened," she said, stirring her latte in tight circles. "I had it. I actually had control. And then it just... evaporated."

This is the part nobody warns you about: that first month of success can actually make the relapse worse. Because now you know what the other side feels like. You've tasted what it's like to go to bed without that low-grade financial anxiety, to check your bank balance without dread, to make choices instead of discovering your decisions like crimes you committed during a blackout.

Getting that control and then losing it again doesn't just cost money. It costs something harder to quantify—the belief that change is actually possible. That you're capable of doing this. That your brain isn't just permanently wired to sabotage your own financial stability.

Every time someone gets to Day 45, hits a rough week, and watches the whole system collapse, it gets harder to convince themselves to try again. The internal monologue shifts from "I'm learning a new skill" to "I'm fundamentally broken at this." And that belief, more than any individual purchase, is what keeps people stuck in the same patterns for decades.

I'm spending time on this because the stakes matter. This isn't about saving an extra fifty bucks in April. This is about whether you're going to spend the next ten years of your life in the same anxious, reactive relationship with money that you're in right now, or whether something fundamental actually changes.

So let's change it.

The mistake Lisa made—the same mistake I made, the same mistake most people make—was treating her February system as a fixed thing. A set of rules she needed to follow indefinitely, with the exact same level of conscious attention forever.

That's exhausting. More importantly, it's wrong.

Think about learning to drive. When you first got behind the wheel, you were consciously managing everything. Check mirror. Signal. Check blind spot. Adjust speed. Maintain lane position. Your brain was running a full diagnostic on every action, and you probably felt mentally wiped after twenty minutes of driving in an empty parking lot.

Nobody drives like that after ten years. The actions become automatic. Your hands adjust the wheel without conscious thought. You check mirrors without mentally noting that you're checking mirrors. The cognitive load drops to almost nothing, which is why you can drive across town while having a conversation and arrive at your destination barely remembering the drive itself.

That's where we're heading with impulse control. Not "stay vigilant forever," but "build new automatic responses that require less and less conscious effort."

The tools you're using right now—the Impulse Tracker, the Pause & Plan script, the daily check-ins—those are training wheels. You're using them to build new neural pathways, new default responses to the cues that usually trigger spending. Eventually, most of this becomes automatic. You see a targeted Instagram ad and your brain runs the pause-and-evaluate process without you consciously invoking it. You feel the urge to buy something and immediately recognize it as stress about tomorrow's presentation, without needing to write it down.

But here's the crucial part: you can't force that automation. You can't skip ahead to month twelve and expect your brain to have built pathways you never practiced. You have to put in the conscious reps first.

The evolution looks different for everyone, but the general pattern holds. Let me walk you through what it actually looks like.

Months 1-3: Everything is manual

This is where Lisa was in February. Where you are now, or about to be. You're actively tracking every impulse. Running through the script word for word. Checking your fun money balance before purchases. Treating this like a skill you're deliberately building, because that's exactly what it is.

This phase is supposed to feel effortful. That's not a bug. That's your brain building new pathways.

David Chen, a software engineer I worked with in Austin, kept his Impulse Tracker as a physical notebook during this phase—the kind with a red cover and graph paper inside. He'd tried phone apps and found them too frictionless, too easy to ignore. The physical notebook lived on his desk, deliberately placed between his monitor and his keyboard. Any time he opened Amazon or browsed Reddit's watch exchange forums (his particular weakness), he had to move the notebook out of the way. That physical interaction created a moment of awareness that digital tracking never did for him.

Sometimes he'd open the notebook, write down what he wanted to buy, and close both the notebook and the browser without purchasing anything. Sometimes he'd complete the entry and buy the thing anyway. Didn't matter. The practice was the point. He was teaching his brain to notice the impulse, to create space between wanting and buying, to treat these urges as data worth examining rather than commands requiring immediate obedience.

The key thing David did right during those first three months? He didn't judge himself for having the impulses. He just observed them. Logged them like weather patterns, not moral failures.

Months 3-6: You start seeing the pattern

This is where it gets interesting, and where most people have their first major breakthrough.

By month three, if you've been consistently tracking, the patterns become almost comically obvious. You'll wonder how you never noticed them before, these clear cause-and-effect relationships between your emotional state and your spending behavior.

For Lisa, once she got back on track in late March and committed to tracking through April and May, the pattern was unmistakable:

every impulse purchase happened in the hour after she'd had a difficult conversation with someone. A tense client call. A fight with her husband. A frustrating back-and-forth with her daughter's school. Within sixty minutes of hanging up or walking away, she'd buy something online. The purchase was never related to the conversation. It was just... what her brain did with the emotional residue.

Once you see the pattern, you can intervene before the impulse even arrives.

Lisa started building in a buffer. Any time she had one of those conversations, she'd set a one-hour timer on her phone labeled "No buying anything." That's it. No complex strategy, no substitute behavior, just a simple rule: give yourself one hour before making any purchase decisions.

Her impulse spending dropped by sixty percent. Not because she'd developed superhuman willpower, but because she'd addressed the actual trigger—the specific emotional state that preceded the urge—instead of just trying to resist the urge once it showed up.

This is the phase where you stop fighting symptoms and start solving causes. You're moving upstream.

And this is where a lot of people get frustrated, because they think awareness should be enough. They've identified the pattern, so they should be able to just... stop doing it. Like consciousness alone creates change. When it doesn't—when they still feel the pull toward spending even though they *know* why it's happening—they interpret that as failure.

It's not failure. Awareness is step one. Changing the conditions that create the impulse is step two. And step three, the one that actually makes this sustainable, is giving yourself something else to do with that energy.

Months 6-12: You build substitutes that actually work

By six months in, you know your triggers. You've probably addressed some of the environmental ones—moved your phone across the room at night, deleted shopping apps, unsubscribed from promotional emails. But you're still human, which means you're still going to have moments of stress, boredom, restlessness, that vague feeling of wanting *something* even if you can't name what.

This is where substitution matters. And I don't mean the standard advice you've heard before, the "go for a walk instead of shopping" suggestions that sound reasonable and feel completely useless when you're actually in the grip of an impulse.

Those suggestions fail because they're not equivalent substitutes. Shopping delivers a very specific reward—the novelty, the anticipation, the dopamine hit of acquisition, the fantasy of how this thing will change your life. Going for a walk delivers none of that.

What works is finding something that hits the same reward system but costs less.

For David, it was Craigslist browsing with no buying allowed.

He'd been spending serious money on watches—vintage Seikos, Soviet-era military pieces, anything mechanical with a story. Not huge amounts per purchase, maybe $80 to $200, but it added up to $400 or $500 some months. The problem wasn't that he loved watches (he did). The problem was that he was buying them impulsively, chasing the thrill of the search and the acquisition, not actually building a meaningful collection.

So he made a rule: he could browse Craigslist for watches any time he wanted. Could spend an hour scrolling through listings, looking at photos, imagining the story behind each piece. But he couldn't contact sellers or make purchases. If he found something he really wanted, he'd bookmark it and sit with that wanting for seventy-two hours. If he still wanted it after three days, and it fit his monthly watch budget ($150, which he'd set deliberately), he could buy it.

What he discovered surprised him: the browsing itself scratched most of the itch. The searching, the evaluating, the imagining—that delivered the dopamine hit he was actually chasing. By the time seventy-two hours passed, he usually didn't care about the watch anymore. The wanting had been satisfied by the browsing, without the purchase.

His watch spending dropped to maybe one purchase every two or three months—only the pieces he genuinely wanted to keep. And he was enjoying the hobby more, because now each purchase felt intentional instead of compulsive.

That's what equivalent substitution means. Find the thing that delivers the same reward structure without the financial cost. It won't be the same for everyone. For some people it's library holds instead of buying books. For others it's window shopping with a strict no-buying rule, or browsing Pinterest boards, or playing video games that simulate the acquisition loop. The specific substitute doesn't matter. What matters is that it genuinely satisfies the same psychological need.

After month 12: Most of it runs on autopilot

Here's the part that actually surprised me when I first did this work myself, years before I ever helped anyone else with it: it genuinely does get easier. Not in a "you'll never be tempted again" way, but in a "the temptation doesn't hijack your entire decision-making process" way.

Lisa, by January—ten months after her March collapse—could walk through Target, which had been her absolute danger zone, and barely register most of the things that would've stopped her cold a year earlier. Not because she'd developed iron willpower. Because her brain had built new default responses.

See attractive thing. Notice the impulse. Auto-evaluate: does this fit my actual priorities right now? Usually no. Move on.

The Impulse Tracker had mostly faded into the background by this point. She'd pull it out occasionally, especially during stressful periods or when she noticed a new pattern emerging. But she wasn't logging every single impulse anymore, because most of them weren't making it past the automatic filter.

The Pause & Plan script was similar. She didn't need to consciously run through it anymore. The structure of it—pause, identify what's actually happening, evaluate whether this aligns with what I want—had become automatic, the way checking your mirrors before changing lanes becomes automatic after enough repetition.

But that automation didn't mean she stopped paying attention entirely. And this is the part that trips people up.

Maintenance isn't about freezing the system in place and following the same practices forever. It's about developing enough self-awareness to notice when things start to slip, and enough flexibility to adjust before it becomes a real problem.

For Lisa, that meant a monthly check-in. She literally put it on her calendar—thirty minutes on the last Sunday of every month, blocked out like a meeting with herself.

The process was simple. Four questions, asked in order.

First: What did the numbers actually do this month?

Not what you *meant* to spend. Not what you *should have* spent according to some ideal budget you set in January. What did you actually spend? Is any category way over what you expected? If so, was it truly unexpected—like, something broke and needed replacing—or is it a slow creep that you didn't notice day-to-day?

This isn't about judgment. It's information. You can't course-correct if you don't know which direction you're drifting.

Lisa noticed in July, for example, that her restaurant spending had jumped. Not drastically, but enough to register—about $180 more than usual. When she looked at the individual charges, she realized she'd been meeting friends for dinner more often. Which was actually a good thing, something she'd been trying to do more of after a pretty isolated spring. But it meant she needed to either adjust her restaurant budget up or consciously choose cheaper places.

She picked option two—started suggesting lunch instead of dinner, or coffee instead of full meals. Restaurant spending came back down, social life stayed active, problem solved. But only because she noticed the drift early enough to do something about it.

Second: Were there any new triggers this month?

Old patterns you thought you'd handled that came back? New situations that created impulses you haven't seen before?

This is where Lisa caught the Instagram-in-bed pattern I mentioned earlier. She'd started a new weekend routine without really thinking about it—scrolling her phone first thing Saturday morning while still under the covers. Harmless enough, except her feed had apparently decided she was in the market for home decor, and she kept seeing these beautiful minimalist bedroom setups that made her current furniture look sad by comparison.

Three Saturdays in a row, she bought something. A throw pillow. A print for the wall. New sheets. None of it expensive, all of it unnecessary, and she didn't even make the connection until the monthly review.

Fix was easy: move the phone across the room before bed on Friday nights. Can't scroll in bed if the phone isn't within reach. Impulse spending dropped back to baseline.

Third: Am I spending money on things that actually matter to me?

This is less concrete than the other questions, but maybe more important in the long run.

Are you putting money toward the things you said you cared about when you started this whole process? Or are you still leaking money toward things that seem important in the moment but don't connect to anything you actually value?

Lisa realized in September that she'd been spending about $120 a month on professional development—online courses, mostly, in marketing and business strategy. Which sounds virtuous, right? Investing in yourself, building skills, all of that.

Except when she actually looked at it honestly, she didn't care that much about marketing theory. She already knew how to run her business. What she actually wanted—what she'd wanted for years but kept putting off—was to take a pottery class. Not for business. Not to build a side income. Just because she thought it would be fun and she missed working with her hands.

So she cut the course budget from $120 to zero and redirected that money to the pottery class. Eight weeks, $280 total. The best $280 she spent all year, because it was aligned with what she actually wanted, not with some imagined version of who she thought she should be.

When your spending aligns with your actual values—not the values you think you're supposed to have, but the ones that are true for you—every other decision gets easier. Because now there's a clear trade-off. Buying those sheets doesn't just mean "spending money I maybe shouldn't spend." It means "less money for the thing I actually care about." Much easier to say no when the stakes are real.

Fourth: Is my fun money amount still right?

Are you consistently running out before the month ends, or consistently rolling over unused money? Either one suggests the amount needs adjusting.

And this is the piece I think most budget advice misses entirely: the goal is not to minimize fun money to zero. The goal is to find the amount that lets you actually enjoy your life without undermining your larger goals.

Lisa's fun money started at $200. Dropped to $150 as she got better at distinguishing between "fun" and "impulse." Then actually went back up to $200 once she'd built her emergency fund to a comfortable level and wanted to allocate more toward experiences with her daughter.

The number itself doesn't matter. What matters is that it's intentional, that it still fits your current life, and that you're willing to revisit it when it stops working.

Let's talk about the thing that derails most people somewhere between month four and month eight: the belief that if you're doing this right, you should never mess up.

You will mess up. Plan on it.

There will be a day when you're exhausted, emotionally raw from something that has nothing to do with money, and you'll buy something you absolutely don't need and maybe don't even want. You'll complete the purchase and immediately feel that familiar sinking guilt. And then you'll face a choice.

You can treat it as confirmation that you're bad at this, that you'll never get it right, that you should just give up and go back to how things were before. A lot of people take that option. It's almost comforting, in a self-destructive way—if you're going to fail anyway, why keep trying?

Or you can treat it as data.

When David bought that $340 watch—the one he saw on Craigslist, bookmarked, told himself he'd wait three days on, and then bought anyway after eighteen hours—he could have spiraled into self-recrimination and given up on the whole system.

Instead, he sat down that same evening and logged it in his notebook. Not just “bought watch, $340,” but the complete context. What had happened that day. What he was feeling. What he thought the watch would do for him emotionally. What specifically broke down in his usual pause-and-evaluate process.

Then he asked himself one question: *What would need to be different for me to make a different choice next time?*

Not “why am I weak,” not “what’s wrong with me.” Just: what would need to change?

For David, the answer was specific. The seventy-two-hour rule wasn’t long enough when he was in a particular emotional state—specifically, when he’d had a frustrating day at work and was looking for any sense of control or accomplishment. So he added a new condition: if he was feeling that specific way, the waiting period extended to a full week. And he had to tell his wife about the thing he wanted to buy, which added a layer of accountability that made impulsive purchases much harder to execute.

That one “failure” became the catalyst for a system adjustment that prevented probably a dozen future impulse purchases.

This is what I mean by treating mistakes as data instead of evidence of personal failure. You’re not trying to be perfect. You’re trying to build a system that works with your actual human brain, complete with all its emotional volatility and irrational impulses.

Progress is the goal. Perfection is a trap.

Here's what I wish someone had told me seven years ago, before I stuck that "Day 30" Post-it on my mirror: the techniques matter, but they're not the actual point.

The Impulse Tracker matters. The Pause & Plan script matters. The fun money account, the monthly review, the trigger audits—all of it matters. These are valuable, practical tools that genuinely help.

But the deeper work, the thing that makes this sustainable for years instead of weeks, is changing your relationship with wanting itself.

Most of us have been taught that wanting is a problem to be solved. Either you give in to every want and end up broke and guilty, or you suppress every want and end up resentful and deprived. Those feel like the only options.

But there's a third way, and it's the one that actually works long-term: you can acknowledge the want, get genuinely curious about it, and let it exist without acting on it.

This was the hardest shift for me personally. I'd spent years treating impulses as either commands I had to obey or enemies I had to fight. Learning to just observe them, the way you might observe clouds moving across the sky, felt almost impossibly difficult at first.

But here's what I eventually discovered, and what Lisa and David both discovered in their own ways: most impulses, if you don't immediately act on them, fade on their own. Usually within ten or fifteen minutes. Sometimes less.

They're not permanent features of your personality. They're temporary mental events, triggered by whatever's happening in your environment and emotional state right now. They arrive, they peak, and if you don't feed them with action, they dissipate.

Lisa started timing this. Literally setting a timer when she felt a strong urge to buy something, just to see how long the urgency lasted. What she found: the overwhelming *need* to purchase whatever she was fixated on usually faded below the threshold of "I have to have this right now" within twelve minutes. Sometimes it came back later, but weaker. And the more times she practiced just letting the impulse arrive and pass without reacting to it, the easier the whole process became.

This isn't meditation advice, though meditation does help with exactly this skill. It's just accurate information about how impulses actually work in your brain. They're temporary. The feeling of "I need this right now" is not a reliable signal about what you actually need. It's just a feeling, and feelings change.

The freedom that comes from really internalizing this—from knowing that you can want something and not buy it, that the wanting won't destroy you or last forever—is hard to overstate. It changes everything.

You know what nobody tells you about long-term maintenance? The real marker of success isn't that you stop wanting things. It's that you stop being afraid of wanting them.

Lisa, about fourteen months in, told me something that stuck with me. She said, "I used to avoid going into stores I liked because I didn't trust myself. Like I was some kind of danger to my own financial stability. Now I can walk through Anthropologie just because I enjoy looking at beautiful things. Sometimes I buy something. Most of the time I don't. Either way is fine."

That's what we're actually building toward. Not a system where you're forever vigilant, forever restricting yourself, forever treating your own desires as threats to be managed.

A system where you can want things, enjoy wanting them, and make actual choices about which wants to act on. Where you trust yourself to make those choices based on what matters to you, not based on whatever emotional state you happen to be in at the moment.

Where you're not at war with yourself anymore.

That's the shift that makes everything else sustainable. And it doesn't happen in month one. It happens slowly, sometimes so slowly you don't notice it's happening until you catch yourself doing something that would've been impossible a year ago—walking past something you want, feeling the pull of it, and choosing to keep walking without any internal drama about it.

The question you're probably sitting with right now is: how do I actually get there from here?

Start with this week. Not the whole year, not even the whole month. Just this week.

What's one pattern you've already noticed in your spending? One trigger that keeps showing up? Pick the most obvious one—the one where the connection between your emotional state and your impulse to spend is so clear you can't ignore it anymore.

Now design one small intervention. Not a complete system overhaul. Just one thing that disrupts that specific pattern. A timer. A physical barrier. A substitution. Something simple enough that you'll actually do it.

Do that for seven days and see what happens.

Then come back next Sunday and ask yourself: did it work? If yes, keep it and add one more intervention for a different pattern. If no, adjust and try again.

You're not trying to fix everything at once. You're trying to prove to yourself that change is possible, that you're capable of building new responses, that this isn't just another thing you'll fail at.

One pattern. One week. One small intervention.

What's waiting on the other side—the version of your life where money isn't this constant source of anxiety, where you make real choices instead of discovering them later in your bank statement—that's worth the slow work of getting there.

The question is: what's the one thing you're going to try this week?

The honest answer is: you'll probably pick something, try it for three days, forget about it by Thursday, and then feel guilty about it two weeks from now when you're reading this chapter again.

That's not pessimism. That's just what happens when you're trying to build new patterns while the rest of your life keeps demanding attention. The rent doesn't care that you're trying to develop financial awareness. Your kid's school registration deadline doesn't wait for you to finish your self-improvement project.

So here's what long-term maintenance actually looks like: it's not a smooth upward trajectory where each week builds perfectly on the last. It's more like a coastline—lots of ins and outs, some stretches where you're making real progress, some stretches where you can't even see the shore.

The difference between people who actually change their relationship with money and people who just keep trying and failing isn't that the successful ones never lose momentum. It's that they know how to restart without making it a whole dramatic thing.

When you notice you've stopped doing your weekly pattern check-in, you don't need to have a reckoning with yourself about why you're so undisciplined. You don't need to start over from scratch. You just need to do it this Sunday. One data point is better than zero data points, and zero data points is better than a guilt spiral that convinces you the whole thing was stupid anyway.

This is where most people lose the plot. They think if they're not doing it perfectly, they're failing. So when they miss a week, they feel like they've broken the streak, and if the streak is broken, what's the point? Might as well wait until next month to start fresh, or next year, or after this stressful period ends.

But maintenance isn't about streaks. It's about density over time. If you do your pattern work three weeks out of four, that's a 75% implementation rate, which is vastly better than the 0% you were operating at before. If you catch yourself repeating an old pattern twice instead of five times in a month, you haven't failed because you didn't eliminate it completely—you've succeeded at reducing it by 60%.

The goal isn't perfection. The goal is a version of your life where you're paying attention more often than you're checked out, where you catch yourself more often than you don't, where the gap between the behavior and the awareness of the behavior gets shorter.

That gap is everything. When you were deep in the pattern, you'd make the impulse purchase and not even realize it was a pattern until you were looking at your credit card statement weeks later. Then maybe you started noticing it the day after. Then a few hours after. Then while you were doing it. Then right before you were about to do it.

Each of those is a different level of awareness, and each one gives you more room to make a different choice. You can't make a different choice if you don't know you're making a choice in the first place.

So when you're thinking about long-term maintenance, you're really thinking about two things: how do I keep the awareness sharp, and how do I not collapse when the awareness shows me something I don't want to see?

Keeping the awareness sharp is the easier part. You need regular check-ins—not because check-ins are magic, but because without them, you default back to autopilot. Weekly works for most people. Monthly is too infrequent; you lose the thread. Daily is too much; it becomes another obligation you resent.

The check-in doesn't need to be elaborate. You're just asking: what did I notice this week about my money patterns? What worked? What didn't? What do I want to try next week?

Some weeks you'll have a lot to say. Some weeks you'll write three sentences and be done. Both are fine. You're just maintaining the habit of looking, because the moment you stop looking is the moment you slide back into the old patterns without realizing it.

The harder part is not collapsing when the awareness shows you something uncomfortable. Because it will. You'll notice that you've been using shopping as a way to avoid dealing with your relationship.

You'll realize that your "I deserve this" purchases are actually "I hate my job and I don't know how to leave" purchases. You'll see that the reason you never have money saved is because some part of you doesn't actually believe you deserve security.

This is the point where a lot of people bail. They came here to fix their budget, not to have feelings about their childhood or their marriage or their sense of self-worth. They wanted a simple problem with a simple solution, and instead they're looking at something that feels too big to touch.

Here's what you do: you touch it anyway, but you touch it small.

You don't have to solve your entire relationship with security. You just have to notice that it's there, and ask yourself: what's one small thing I could do this week that would be me acting like someone who deserves security? Maybe it's moving $20 into savings. Maybe it's actually reading the letter from your insurance company instead of letting it sit on the counter for three weeks. Maybe it's just saying out loud, "I'm avoiding this because it scares me," instead of pretending you forgot.

Small acts of acknowledgment are surprisingly powerful. You're not fixing the thing yet. You're just proving to yourself that you can look at it without falling apart, that you can name it without being destroyed by it.

And over time—months, not weeks—you start to notice that the thing that felt too big to touch has gotten smaller, or maybe you've gotten bigger, or maybe both. The awareness that used to feel like an accusation starts to feel like information. The patterns that used to feel like proof of your brokenness start to feel like old strategies that made sense once but don't anymore.

That's what maintenance looks like in the long term. Not a finished product. Not a solved problem. Just a slowly shifting relationship where you have more room to move, more capacity to choose, more ability to see what's actually happening instead of what you're afraid is happening.

You're still going to mess up. You're still going to have months where everything falls apart. You're still going to sometimes choose the old pattern even when you can see it coming.

But you'll also have months where you don't. Where you catch yourself mid-pattern and choose differently. Where you notice you're anxious about money and instead of spending to numb it, you sit with it long enough to figure out what it's actually about.

Those months are the proof. Not that you've arrived, but that you're building something real.

The Post-it note is still there. 'Day 30' in green Sharpie. I see it every morning. What I don't see anymore is the feeling I had when I wrote it—that I'd crossed a finish line. Because here's what I know now: there is no finish line.

Chapter 9: Your Impulse Control Toolkit

Open your phone right now. Go to your subscriptions. Scroll through the list. How many apps are you paying for that you've forgotten existed? I have eleven. Forty-three dollars a month. That's the money—but it's also the symptom.

Remember MealFlow Premium from Chapter 2—the app I bought while teaching people not to buy apps? It's in my 'Things I Almost Deleted' folder now, right next to ten others. The folder isn't about the money. It's about the pattern.

I started the folder three years ago after a particularly brutal month where I spent $800 on stuff I couldn't account for. Not big purchases. No single thing that made me gasp when I saw my credit card statement. Just... bleeding. A $40 here, a $65 there. Books I didn't read. Gadgets I used once. A pair of running shoes when I already owned two pairs that were perfectly fine and I wasn't even running regularly.

The folder now has 347 screenshots. You know how many of those things I actually bought after waiting 48 hours?

Maybe thirty.

I'm telling you this because I want you to know that I'm not writing this chapter from some imaginary high ground where I figured it all out and now I'm here to bestow wisdom upon you from my throne of perfect financial discipline. I'm writing it from the trenches. From the same place you are, where you *know* what you should do, you've *read* about what you should do, and yet somehow you still end up sitting in your car wondering how you just spent $143 on throw pillows when you came in for detergent.

The gap between knowing and doing—that's where we live. That's the terrain we're mapping in this chapter.

And here's what I've learned, the hard way, over years of trying and failing and trying again: you can't willpower your way across that gap. You need tools. Actual, functional, boring tools that work even when you don't feel like it. Especially when you don't feel like it.

That's what this chapter is. Your toolkit. The stuff that actually works when everything else—the motivation, the fresh-start energy, the promise you made to yourself last Sunday that *this* time would be different—runs out.

Let's start with something that might sound obvious but is absolutely foundational, the thing I wish someone had told me years ago instead of letting me figure it out through expensive trial and error:

You cannot manage what you do not measure.

I know. It sounds like a motivational poster you'd see in a dentist's office, right next to the one about how "A smile is a curve that sets everything straight." But stay with me, because this is the part where most people get it wrong.

When I say "measure," I don't mean track your spending after the fact. I don't mean adding up receipts at the end of the month and seeing where your money went. That's useful, sure—it's an autopsy. It tells you what happened. But you can't change what already happened.

What we're doing is different. We're tracking the *moment before*. The urge itself. The impulse before it becomes a purchase.

Think of it like this: if you were trying to lose weight, you wouldn't just weigh yourself once a month and hope for the best, right? You'd pay attention to *when* you were eating, *why* you were eating, what you were feeling right before you reached for the snack you didn't actually want but ate anyway because it was there and you were bored or stressed or just... feeling something you didn't want to feel.

Same principle. We're tracking the emotional weather patterns that lead to impulse spending. And we're doing it in real time, not in hindsight when your memory has already smoothed over the details and reconstructed the story in a way that makes you feel better about it.

I call this the **Impulse Spending Audit**, and before you roll your eyes at the word "audit"—I know, it sounds tedious, it sounds like homework, it sounds like the opposite of fun—let me tell you what happened when Sarah did this for just one week.

Sarah. Same Sarah who spent eleven minutes in the Target parking lot back at the beginning of this chapter, surrounded by bags full of stuff she didn't need and a crushing sense that maybe she was just fundamentally broken in some way that made this whole impulse-control thing impossible for her.

She ran the audit. Seven days. Every time she felt the urge to buy something unplanned—not after she bought it, *as she was feeling it*—she wrote down three things:

What was happening around her. The setup. The scenery. Where she was, what time it was, what she'd been doing five minutes before the urge hit. Was she scrolling? Working? Procrastinating? Alone or with people? Had something just happened—a stressful email, a compliment, an argument, a moment of feeling left out or behind or inadequate?

What triggered the specific urge *right then*. The thing that made her reach for her wallet in that exact moment. An ad. A sale notification. A friend showing up with something new. A package arriving at a neighbor's door, making her realize she hadn't gotten any packages lately and suddenly that felt like a problem that needed solving. (Yes, really. She wrote that one down. The absence of packages felt like deprivation. We are living in a deeply strange time.)

What she was feeling. Before, during, and after. This is the part that matters most, and it's the part people skip because it's uncomfortable. Nobody wants to write down "I felt inadequate and buying this made me feel like I was doing something about it, even though I knew it wouldn't actually help." But that's exactly what you need to write down. The truth, not the story you tell yourself later.

End of the week, Sarah had seventeen entries. Seventeen moments where she almost bought something, or did buy something, or stood in a store aisle trying to talk herself out of buying something while her brain generated increasingly creative justifications for why this particular candle was actually an investment in her wellbeing.

(Sidenote: I have a theory that we collectively decided "self-care" could mean literally anything we wanted it to mean, and now every purchase under $50 is self-care. Candles are self-care. Throw pillows are self-care. The $38 face serum is self-care. That subscription box you'll forget about is self-care. We've turned the whole concept into a permission slip to buy whatever we want without guilt. But I digress.)

Here's what Sarah's audit revealed—and this is where it gets interesting, because her pattern was *not* the pattern I expected:

She didn't spend when she was bored. She didn't spend when she saw ads. She didn't even spend much when she was actively scrolling social media, which is supposed to be the big danger zone, right? Influencers and targeted ads and all that.

Sarah spent when she felt stuck.

Specifically: stuck in her work. Stuck on a project. Stuck in a creative problem she didn't know how to solve. And in those moments, buying something—anything—made her feel like she was moving forward. Like she was solving *a* problem, even if it wasn't *the* problem.

Fonts. Desk organizers. Notebooks. A lamp that promised to reduce eye strain. A course on productivity systems. A different chair. A keyboard that supposedly increased typing speed. She wasn't buying these things because she needed them. She was buying the feeling of progress when the actual progress—the creative work, the hard work, the work that required her to sit with discomfort and not-knowing—felt impossible.

The purchases were fake progress. Expensive theater. And they worked, sort of, for about fifteen minutes. Long enough for her brain to get the little hit of dopamine from solving something. Not long enough to actually help with the real problem.

Once she saw the pattern—once she could name it—everything changed.

Not because awareness magically fixed it. I need to be really clear about this: knowing why you do something does not automatically give you the power to stop doing it. If it did, nobody would smoke, nobody would doomscroll at 2 AM, nobody would stay in relationships that slowly hollowed them out from the inside. Awareness is necessary. It is not sufficient.

But it gave her something she didn't have before: specific intelligence. She knew *her* pattern. Not the generic advice-column pattern. Not what works for other people. *Her* pattern. And that meant she could build defenses that actually matched the threat.

When she felt stuck, she started going for a walk. Ten minutes, around the block. No phone. Just walking. It sounds stupidly simple, and it didn't work every time, but it worked enough. The urge to buy something would fade, or at least lose its urgency, and by the time she got back to her desk, she could either tackle the problem with fresh eyes or at least sit with the discomfort of being stuck without needing to immediately solve it with a package arriving at her door.

That's what the audit does. It gives you specific intelligence. And specific intelligence gives you specific solutions, not generic advice that may or may not apply to you.

So here's what you're going to do. And yes, I'm assigning homework. I know you probably didn't sign up for homework when you bought this book. But you also didn't sign up for spending $800 a month on stuff you don't remember buying, so here we are.

For one week—seven days, starting whenever you decide to start (though if you're thinking "I'll start Monday" and today isn't Monday, I'm gently suggesting that "I'll start Monday" is the procrastination you tell yourself because starting *right now* feels too immediate and uncomfortable, and maybe you should just start right now)—you're going to track every impulse. Not every purchase. Every *impulse*.

The moment you feel the urge to buy something you didn't plan to buy, you write down three things:

The Setup. Time, place, what you were doing, what happened five minutes before. Be specific. Not "I was on my phone." What were you doing on your phone? Scrolling Instagram? Texting someone? Avoiding something else you didn't want to do? Had you just gotten bad news, good news, no news? Were you alone? Tired? Hungry? (Seriously, "hungry" shows up in these audits way more than it should. If you're someone who shops when you're hungry, that's actionable intelligence. Eat first, shop later.)

The Trigger. The specific thing that made you want to buy *right now*. The ad, the email, the "last chance" notification, the influencer unboxing video, the friend with the new thing, the feeling that everyone else is moving forward and you're standing still. The more specific, the better. You're collecting data. You're not judging yourself. You're just writing down what's true.

The Feeling. What are you feeling before the urge hits? What do you hope buying the thing will make you feel? What do you actually feel during the purchase—if you go through with it—and what do you feel five minutes after?

This part is uncomfortable. Most people want to skip it. Don't. This is where the real intelligence lives. Because once you see that you're not actually buying the candle, you're buying a brief respite from feeling behind or inadequate or stressed, you can start asking: is there a cheaper way to get that feeling? A more effective way? A way that doesn't leave you staring at your bank account at the end of the month wondering where everything went?

You're probably thinking: *Okay, but this sounds like a lot of work. I barely have time to breathe. Now I have to journal every time I want to buy something?*

Fair. It is work. I'm not going to pretend it's effortless.

But let me ask you this: how much time do you spend each month looking at your bank account, trying to figure out where your money went? How much mental energy do you burn feeling guilty about purchases you barely remember making? How many hours do you lose to scrolling, tempted, adding things to your cart, removing them, adding them back, trying to talk yourself out of it or into it, stuck in this exhausting loop of wanting and resisting and wanting again?

You're spending the time either way. Either you spend it now, getting smarter, or you spend it later, feeling bad about yourself. One of those paths leads somewhere. The other just leads to more of the same.

I ran my own audit three years ago, and I learned something I didn't expect: most of my impulse spending happened between 2 PM and 4 PM on weekdays. That stupid afternoon slump. My energy would crash, my focus would dissolve, and suddenly I'd be online, scrolling, looking for something—anything—to give me a little spark of interest or excitement or progress.

I wasn't buying because I needed things. I was buying because I needed to feel something other than the low-grade malaise of a boring Wednesday afternoon where nothing was going right and I couldn't focus and I felt like I was wasting my life one distracted hour at a time.

Once I knew that, I could do something about it. I started taking an actual break at 2:30. Not a "scroll on my phone" break. A real break. I'd go outside. Walk around the block. Get coffee. Talk to a human. Something that interrupted the pattern before the urge even started.

Did it work every time? No. Some days I still found myself with a cart full of stuff I didn't need, trying to justify why *this* time it was different. But it worked enough. And "enough" is what we're aiming for here. Not perfection. Not some impossible standard where you never have an impulse again. Just... enough. Enough that you're not bleeding $800 a month. Enough that you feel like you have some agency in the decision, instead of being yanked around by every ad and notification and fleeting feeling.

That's what the audit gives you: enough.

Now let's talk about the **24-Hour Rule**, because this is the tool that does the most heavy lifting once you've identified your patterns.

The rule is simple: if it's not on your pre-approved list, and it costs more than $25, it goes in the penalty box for 24 hours.

That's it. You don't say no. You don't deny yourself. You don't white-knuckle your way through resisting the urge. You just say: *not yet*.

Add it to a wishlist. Screenshot it. Write it on a piece of paper. Put it in your cart but don't check out. Whatever works for you. Then close the tab, put down your phone, and walk away.

Come back in 24 hours. If you still want it, buy it. No guilt. No justification needed. It survived the waiting period. It's yours.

But here's what actually happens most of the time, and this is the part that still surprises me even though I've seen it over and over again, both in my own life and in the lives of people who've tried this:

The urge fades.

Not because you talk yourself out of it. Not because you develop some kind of monk-like discipline overnight. But because most impulse purchases are powered by urgency, and urgency has a short half-life. The "limited time offer" pressure, the "only 3 left in stock" scarcity, the feeling that you need to act *right now* or miss out forever—that's all manufactured. It's designed to bypass the part of your brain that asks rational questions like "Do I actually need this?" or "Where is this going to go when I get it home?"

Remove the time pressure, and suddenly there's space for those questions to surface.

Sarah started using the 24-hour rule in week two. First week, she tracked. Second week, she added the delay.

She saved sixteen things to her wishlist that week. You know how many she actually bought?

Three.

And all three were things she'd been casually thinking about for weeks before she happened to see them on sale. They weren't impulse grabs. They were real wants that survived the waiting period and turned out to actually improve her life in some small, tangible way. A water bottle that kept her coffee hot, which meant she drank her coffee instead of letting it go cold and then feeling wasteful. A specific brand of pens she'd been meaning to try. A phone stand for her desk that actually did reduce the neck pain she'd been ignoring for months.

The other thirteen? She either forgot about them entirely—like, looked at her wishlist three days later and thought *what even is this, why did I save this*—or she remembered them and couldn't reconstruct the feeling that made her want them in the first place. The urgency was gone. And without the urgency, the want evaporated.

That's over $300 saved in one week. Not through deprivation. Not through some miserable exercise in self-denial. Just through delay. Just through giving her brain enough time to catch up to her impulse.

Here's the thing nobody tells you about the 24-hour rule, though: it doesn't feel good in the moment.

When you're in the grip of the urge, when you've found the thing and it's on sale and there are only three left and the discount ends at midnight, adding it to a wishlist and walking away feels *terrible*. It feels like you're losing. Like you're being punished. Like some joyless taskmaster is saying "no" and you're just supposed to accept it.

That feeling is real. I'm not going to tell you it's not. But I am going to tell you that it passes. Fast. Fifteen minutes, maybe twenty. And then it's just... gone. You forget you even wanted the thing.

The urge was never about the thing itself. It was about the *feeling* the thing promised to deliver. And feelings are fleeting. They change. They dissolve. They get replaced by other feelings, other urges, other distractions.

The thing, though—the thing is permanent. Or at least semi-permanent. You buy it, it shows up, now you own it. Now you have to figure out where it goes. Now it's clutter. Now it's one more thing you have to manage, maintain, remember you bought. Now it's a number on your credit card statement that you have to account for, reconcile, justify to yourself or your partner or whoever else cares about where your money goes.

The feeling passes. The thing stays. That asymmetry is the whole problem.

The 24-hour rule corrects for that. It matches the duration of the decision to the duration of the consequence. You're not making a permanent choice based on a temporary feeling. You're giving the feeling time to pass, and then making the choice from a steadier place.

Does it work every time? No. Sometimes you'll come back 24 hours later and still want the thing, and sometimes you'll buy it, and sometimes it'll turn out to be a waste of money anyway. That's fine. We're not trying to achieve perfection here. We're trying to reduce the volume of regret. We're trying to shift the ratio so that more of your purchases are things you actually wanted, not things you wanted to want.

Let's talk about the **Fun Money Account**, because this is the structure that holds everything else together, and if you skip this part or implement it halfway, the rest of the toolkit is going to feel like you're trying to build a house on sand.

You've probably heard some version of this advice before. Pay yourself first. Set aside money for guilt-free spending. Give every dollar a job. All the personal finance people say some version of it.

Here's why it usually doesn't work:

People set the amount too low.

They look at their spending, feel horrified by how much they've been spending on "unnecessary" stuff, and decide that starting *right now*, they're going to become a different person. A disciplined person. A person who only spends $50 a month on fun stuff, because that's what a responsible adult would do, right?

Then they blow through $50 in the first four days. Maybe less. And they feel like failures. And they decide the whole system doesn't work. And they abandon it. And they go back to spending whatever they were spending before, except now they also feel bad about themselves.

We're not doing that.

Here's how you actually set the amount: you look at what you spent last month on unplanned, impulse, fun-but-unnecessary purchases. Not what you *wish* you'd spent. Not what you *should* have spent if you were a better, more disciplined version of yourself. What you *actually* spent.

If you don't know—and most people don't, because who actually tracks this stuff before they have to—take your best guess. Look at your bank statement. Add up everything that wasn't bills, groceries, gas, or other fixed necessities. What's left? That's your starting number.

Let's say it's $400.

That's your Fun Money Account budget. Not $50. Not $100. $400. The actual number.

I can already hear the objection: *But that's too much! I'm trying to save money, not give myself permission to keep spending it!*

I know. But here's the thing: you're spending $400 either way. Right now, that $400 is bleeding out invisibly, mixed in with your regular spending, impossible to track or contain. It's $40 here, $60 there, oh look another $35, what even was that, I don't remember.

What we're doing is *containing* it. We're building a fence around it. This $400 goes into a separate account, and that's your impulse money. When it's gone, it's gone. No borrowing from other categories. No justifying why *this* purchase should come out of groceries or gas or your emergency fund.

The goal right now is not to spend less. The goal is to *see* your spending clearly, and to make sure it stays in its lane and doesn't crash into the rest of your financial life.

Once you've got that working—once you've gone a month or two and successfully kept your impulse spending contained to the Fun Money Account, no spillover, no overdrafts, no middle-of-the-month panic where you realize you can't actually afford groceries because you spent the money on throw pillows—*then* you can start experimenting with lowering the amount.

Month three, try $350. See how it feels. If it feels manageable, great. If it feels like deprivation, if you're constantly running out and feeling resentful, bump it back up to $375. Find the number that works. The number where you feel like you have enough freedom to breathe, but not so much freedom that you're hemorrhaging money you need for other things.

This is not a one-size-fits-all number. I've seen people who are perfectly happy with $100 a month. I've seen people who need $600 to not feel deprived. It depends on your income, your baseline lifestyle, your specific pattern of spending. The point is not to match some external standard of what a "good" person would spend. The point is to find *your* sustainable number.

Sarah started with $250. That was her real number from the previous month, rounded up a little because she knew she was probably forgetting some purchases.

First month, she spent $230. Under budget. She felt like a champion.

Second month, she spent $290. Over budget by $40. But instead of spiraling into guilt and abandoning the system, she just... made a note. Okay. $250 might be slightly too tight. Let's try $275 next month.

Third month, $260. Under budget again.

By month four, she had a sense of what her actual sustainable number was, and it wasn't $50 or $100 or some aspirational fantasy number. It was around $250-$275. That was the amount where she could buy the occasional thing that made her happy without feeling deprived, and without wrecking her ability to pay rent or save for the actual goals she cared about.

And here's the thing that surprised her: once she knew she *had* $250 to spend, guilt-free, no justification needed, the urgency around individual purchases faded. She didn't feel like she had to grab everything right now because who knew when she'd be "allowed" to buy something again. She could be more selective. She could pass on the mediocre thing because she knew a better version might show up next week, and she'd still have money to spend on it.

Scarcity makes you desperate. Abundance—even modest, contained abundance—makes you choosy.

That's what the Fun Money Account does. It turns you from someone who grabs at everything because you're afraid you'll never get another chance, into someone who can afford to wait for the thing you actually want.

Now let's talk about **friction**, because this is the tool that operates quietly in the background, doing work you don't even notice until you look back and realize how much easier everything got.

Friction is anything that makes an action slightly harder to do. Not impossible. Not locked behind a vault you'd need a safecracker to open. Just... slightly less convenient. Slightly more annoying. Slightly more effort than the effortless, one-click, saved-payment-info, package-arriving-in-two-hours ease that modern commerce has optimized for.

Here's what friction looks like in practice:

Deleting your saved payment info. Every site, every app, every place you've ever bought something online and checked the little box that says "save for next time"—go in and delete it. All of it. Yes, it's tedious. Yes, you'll have to re-enter your card number every time you want to buy something. That's the point. The thirty seconds it takes to get up, find your wallet, pull out your card, type in the numbers—that's thirty seconds where your brain has time to ask, "Wait, do I actually want this?"

Unsubscribing from marketing emails. Every single one. If you bought something once and now they email you three times a week with sales and offers and limited-time deals, unsubscribe. You’re not missing out on deals. You’re removing the slot machine from your pocket. Every email is a pull of the lever, a little hit of temptation. You don’t need that. Nobody needs that.

Removing shopping apps from your phone. Amazon, Target, Etsy, whatever your particular weakness is—delete the app. You can still access the site through a browser if you actually need something. But removing the app means you can’t just tap the icon out of boredom or habit. You have to open the browser, type in the URL, log in. Three extra steps. That’s all it takes to interrupt the autopilot.

Using cash for discretionary spending. This one sounds ancient, I know. Like something your grandmother would suggest. But it works, and the reason it works is simple: cash is *real* in a way that digital numbers on a screen are not. When you hand over $40 in actual paper bills, you feel it. When you tap a card or click “buy now,” you don’t. The pain of paying is abstract, distant, something you’ll deal with later when the bill comes.

Sarah tried the cash thing for one month. She took out $250 in cash at the beginning of the month—her Fun Money budget—and put it in an envelope. That was her impulse money. When it was gone, it was gone.

She hated it.

She told me it felt restrictive, old-fashioned, like she was being punished for not being good enough with digital money. She felt embarrassed pulling out cash at stores when everyone else was tapping their phones. She felt like she was making a big deal out of something that shouldn’t be a big deal.

But it worked.

She spent $180 that month. Under budget by $70. And when I asked her why, she said it wasn't because she was trying to be disciplined or depriving herself. It was because every time she reached for the envelope, she could *see* how much was left. She could see the bills getting thinner. She could feel the weight of the money in her hand before she decided to part with it.

With digital spending, there's no weight. There's no visual cue. You could have $1,000 in your account or $100, and the experience of spending $40 feels exactly the same. It's just a number going down. It doesn't *mean* anything until you run out and suddenly your card declines and you realize you miscalculated somewhere along the way.

Cash makes it real. Cash makes you reckon with the fact that money is a finite resource, and when you spend it on this, you don't have it for that.

Now, I'm not saying you have to use cash forever. Sarah went back to digital after two months because she found it too inconvenient, and that's fine. The point wasn't to punish herself with inconvenience. The point was to reset her relationship with spending, to re-train her brain to feel the weight of the decision before she made it.

Once you've done that—once you've felt what it's like to watch your money physically shrink in your hands—you can go back to digital with a different awareness. You don't forget that the money is real just because you can't see it anymore.

Here's the part I almost didn't include in this chapter, because it feels too personal, maybe too raw. But I think it matters. I think it's the thing that makes the difference between understanding this intellectually and actually *changing* how you relate to money and spending and impulse and control.

The reason we buy stuff we don't need isn't because we're broken or weak or lacking in discipline.

It's because we're trying to solve real problems with the wrong tools.

You're stressed. Buying something gives you a sense of control, of agency, of doing *something* when everything else feels like it's happening to you and you're just along for the ride.

You're bored. Buying something gives you a little spark of novelty, a little hit of "something is happening," when your life feels flat and repetitive and like you're just going through the motions.

You're feeling inadequate. Buying something makes you feel like you're investing in yourself, improving yourself, becoming the kind of person who owns nice things and has their life together, even if the thing itself doesn't actually change anything except the balance in your checking account.

These are real problems. The mistake isn't in trying to solve them. The mistake is in thinking that buying stuff will solve them.

It won't. It never does. Not for longer than the time it takes for the package to arrive and the thrill to wear off and the reality to settle in that you're the same person with the same problems, except now you also have a throw pillow you don't need and less money than you had before.

If you're stressed, you need rest. Or boundaries. Or a different job, or a conversation you've been avoiding, or therapy, or a friend who listens without trying to fix you. You don't need a candle.

If you're bored, you need stimulation that actually engages you. A project. A hobby. A book that makes you think. A walk in a place you've never been. A conversation that surprises you. You don't need another thing to scroll through on your phone.

If you're feeling inadequate, you need to reckon with the gap between who you are and who you think you should be, and you need to either close that gap through real work or make peace with the gap and stop measuring yourself against an imaginary standard that nobody actually meets. You don't need to buy your way into worthiness.

I know that's hard to hear. I know it's easier to buy the thing and feel better for twenty minutes than it is to sit with the discomfort of a real problem that doesn't have an easy solution.

But here's the other side of that: every time you buy the thing instead of facing the problem, you're training your brain that the thing is the solution. You're deepening the groove. You're making it harder to break the pattern next time.

And eventually—maybe not today, maybe not this month, but eventually—you're going to run out of money, or space, or patience with yourself. And you're still going to have the same problems you've always had, except now they're buried under a pile of stuff you don't need and can't return.

The toolkit in this chapter—the audit, the 24-hour rule, the Fun Money Account, the friction—these are tools for interrupting the pattern. For giving yourself space to ask: what am I actually trying to solve here? And is there a better way to solve it than buying something?

Sometimes the answer is no. Sometimes you just want the thing, and that's fine. The Fun Money Account exists for exactly that reason. You get to want things. You get to buy things. You're not a monk.

But sometimes the answer is yes. Sometimes there's a real problem underneath the urge, and if you can see it clearly, you can solve it in a way that actually works. In a way that doesn't leave you sitting in a parking lot eleven minutes after the fact, wondering what the hell just happened and why you can't seem to get this right.

You can get this right. You just need the right tools. And now you have them.

Here's what I want you to do in the next 24 hours—not next week, not when you feel ready, but in the next 24 hours:

Pick one tool from this chapter and implement it. Just one.

Set up the Fun Money Account. Or delete your saved payment info from the three sites you spend the most money on. Or unsubscribe from ten marketing emails. Or start the audit—just for today, just tracking the urges you feel before you act on them.

Don't try to do everything at once. Don't try to overhaul your entire financial life in one ambitious burst of motivation that's going to fizzle out by Thursday. Just pick one thing. The smallest thing. The thing that feels the most doable right now, in this moment, before you close this book and go back to whatever you were doing before you started reading.

Because here's the truth: you already know what to do. You knew before you started this chapter. The gap isn't knowledge. The gap is action.

And action doesn't start with a perfect plan or ideal circumstances or waiting until you feel motivated. Action starts with one small, imperfect step in the direction you want to go.

So take it. Right now. One tool. Twenty-four hours.

And then, once that's working—once it's not perfect, but it's working, it's in place, it's no longer something you have to think about every single day—come back and add another one.

You're not building a system overnight. You're building a life that works, one small tool at a time. And the life you're building is worth more than anything you could ever buy.

Also in the Series

Every book in Money Reset stands on its own — read them in any order. If this one was useful, the library continues:

Tax Strategies to Keep What You Earn

Salary Negotiation Before You Sign

Budgeting for People Who Hate Budgeting

Budgeting From Zero

Budgeting on an Irregular Income

Couples Budgeting

Budgeting After Debt

Budgeting for the Broke Paycheck

Budgeting Without a Spreadsheet

Budgeting for a Bigger Life

www.ingramcontent.com/pod-product-compliance
Lightning Source LLC
LaVergne TN
LVHW010723061126
851857LV00014B/1315
* 9 7 8 1 8 0 4 2 8 2 6 5 6 *